The Strange Career
of Marihuana

The Strange Career of Marihuana

POLITICS AND IDEOLOGY OF DRUG CONTROL IN AMERICA

Jerome L. Himmelstein

CONTRIBUTIONS IN POLITICAL SCIENCE, NUMBER 94

GREENWOOD PRESS
WESTPORT, CONNECTICUT • *LONDON, ENGLAND*

HV
5822
M3
H55
1983

Library of Congress Cataloging in Publication Data

Himmelstein, Jerome L.
  The strange career of marihuana.

  (Contributions in political science, ISSN 0147-1066 ;
no. 94)
  Bibliography: p.
  Includes index.
  1. Marihuana. 2. Narcotics, Control of—United States
—History. 3. Marihuana—Law and legislation—United
States. I. Title. II. Series.
HV5822.M3H55 1983   363.4'5   82-12181
ISBN 0-313-23517-1 (lib. bdg.)

Library of Congress Catalog Card Number: 82-12181
ISBN: 0-313-23517-1
ISSN: 0147-1066

First published in 1983

Greenwood Press
A division of Congressional Information Service, Inc.
88 Post Road West
Westport, Connecticut 06881

Printed in the United States of America

10 9 8 7 6 5 4 3 2 1

$27.95

MAR 3 1984

TO THE MEMORY
OF MY FATHER

CONTENTS

FIGURE AND TABLES

FIGURE

TABLES

ACKNOWLEDGMENTS

Many persons have shared in my thinking and contributed to my research on drug controls over the past few years. Special thanks must go first to Harry Levine and Patricia Morgan, with whom I have discussed my ideas continuously since the mid-1970s. For several years our meetings provided the framework within which our respective writings unfolded: Harry's on the ideology of the Temperance Movement in nineteenth-century America, Pat's on the history of narcotics control in California, and my own on marihuana. I appreciate their care, criticism, and support.

Several others also deserve thanks for reading drafts of my work and providing suggestions and encouragement at crucial moments: Don Cahalan, Troy Duster, William Gamson, Jerry Mandel, Gary Marx, Ron Roizen, Robin Room, Jerome Skolnick, Guy Swanson, and Mayer Zald. In addition, I am grateful to Joyce Gordon, Mary Hartness, Carol Seiden, Janet Somers, Sheila Wilder, and Susan Urquhart, who at various stages helped produce the manuscript.

I conducted the initial research for this book with the support of research training fellowships from the U.S. National Institute on Alcohol Abuse and Alcoholism (AA00037) and from the State of California, Office of Alcoholism (ALC 34012-6), administered by the Social Research Group, School of Public Health, University of California, Berkeley. Subsequent work and preparation of the final manuscript were carried out while I was participating in a U.S. National Institute of Mental Health training program in sociology, social policy, and the professions (MH-14598) at the Center for Research on Social Organization at the University of Michigan, Ann Arbor.

Beyond material support, the Social Research Group and the Center for Research on Social Organization provided me with sympathetic, interesting colleagues and a supportive atmosphere within which to work. Many persons at both research institutes have contributed to my intellectual life.

To the close friends who have sustained me over these several years, thanks are, of course, superfluous. And to Evelyn Bogen, who has shared my life, what can mere words say?

The Strange Career
of Marihuana

THE STRANGE   1
CAREER OF MARIHUANA

THE ISSUES

President Franklin Roosevelt signed the Marihuana Tax Act into
law on August 2, 1937, effectively making the use and sale of marihuana federal offenses. Forty years later to the day, President
Jimmy Carter officially proposed to decriminalize marihuana—to
remove criminal penalties for its use and for the nonprofit transfer
of small amounts of it, while maintaining penalties for trafficking.

The two events represent two major phases in the strange career
of marihuana in the United States in the twentieth century. Prior
to the mid-1960s, marihuana use was small and concentrated among
marginal social groups—at various times Mexican laborers, poor
blacks, jazz musicians, and beatniks. In the 1960s, use expanded
rapidly, spreading in particular to middle-class youth in the suburbs
and on college campuses. The cutting point between the two phases
can be taken as 1964, the year in which this change was first publicly
announced in magazine articles with titles such as "Dope Invades
the Suburbs" and "The College Drug Scene."[1]

As the pattern of marihuana use changed, the moral and legal
career of marihuana took a sharp turn as well. The decades prior
to the 1960s had witnessed the outlawing of the possession and sale
of the drug on both state and federal levels and the progressive
escalation of penalties for both offenses. These measures had been

justified by a public image of marihuana as a "killer weed" that turned its users into violent criminals. During this time, marihuana use had been a minor public issue in the United States; but when people had considered it, they had agreed that the drug was indeed evil and that a policy of criminal sanctions was appropriate.

The second phase of marihuana history, from 1964 to the mid-1970s, saw the crumbling of this consensus and the partial reform of the laws that were based on it. There was no longer any agreement on the dangers of the drug or the legitimacy of criminal sanctions against it. Some maintained that marihuana was indeed a public menace, while others dismissed that time-honored image of the drug as so much superstition and exaggeration. Some argued that marihuana laws needed only minor changes, while others demanded substantial, thoroughgoing reform.

Out of this conflict, a new legal direction and ideological consensus emerged. Possession of marihuana for use was reduced from a felony to a misdemeanor in most places and was decriminalized in eleven states. Even the staunchest opponents of penalty reduction generally agreed that mere users, despite their lawbreaking acts, ought not to be regarded as "criminals" or subjected to actual imprisonment; those who wanted penalties kept on the books often argued for a *de facto* decriminalization in which the penalties were not likely to be applied.

Despite the disagreement over the danger of sustained marihuana use, the possibility of moderate, limited use with minimal ill effect was recognized widely for the first time. A new distinction arose between "social," or "experimental," users and "heavy" users. Among those who regarded marihuana as dangerous, moreover, a dramatically altered image of that danger emerged: Marihuana was no longer described as a "killer weed" that fostered aggression and violence but as a "drop-out drug" that sapped users' wills, destroyed their motivation, and turned them into passive drop-outs from reality and society.

In short, from the mid-1960s to the mid-1970s, immense changes occurred not only in the marihuana laws but also, and more importantly, in the entire framework of assumptions within which the drug and the laws were publicly discussed. Marihuana, its users, and the laws controlling it were seen in new terms.

Since the mid-1970s, the movement for further reforms in laws on marihuana has all but died—a victim of the broader, more conservative drift of American politics. Most penalty reductions remain on the books, however, and the marihuana issue still is debated largely in the terms set down in the late 1960s and early 1970s.

We shall attempt to document and explain these changes by providing an overview of the history of marihuana control in the United States in the twentieth century. Our purpose is not to present a detailed narrative of events but to explain important features of that history, to answer the whys and hows, not the whats. We are engaged, in other words, in historical sociology, not history.

Much has been written about marihuana laws, and this ample literature has focused on two issues: the genesis of the Marihuana Tax Act of 1937 and the tumultuous debate over marihuana since the 1960s. In each case, two major hypotheses have dominated discussions. The Marihuana Tax Act has been understood either as the product of the moralistic, expansionist activity of the Federal Bureau of Narcotics, the agency then responsible for enforcing America's drug laws, or as the result of political pressure based on grass-roots anti-Mexican sentiment. Growing support for marihuana law reform since the 1960s has been tied to the increase in middle-class use, while opposition to the drug has been linked to marihuana's role as a symbol of the political and cultural rebellion of youth in the late 1960s and early 1970s, the Counterculture. We shall examine critically all four of these claims. We shall see how both accounts of the genesis of the Marihuana Tax Act are mistaken; we shall refine the understanding of how the changed social status of marihuana users influenced law reform; and we shall learn exactly how marihuana acted as a symbol of youthful rebellion.

Compared to the considerable attention given to marihuana laws, relatively little has been said about marihuana ideology, the terms in which the drug and the laws have been publicly discussed and justified. Here "public discussion" refers not to popular opinion as recorded in survey research, for example, but rather to discourse on marihuana formally open to common or general view—in particular, what has been said about the drug in government hearings and reports and in the communications media. We shall trace how the dominant assumptions about marihuana, its users, and the law developed and changed in public discussion from the 1890s to the mid-1970s. In particular, we shall examine the evolving image of the drug itself and the changing array of arguments made about marihuana laws.

We shall also make certain broader points about marihuana ideology and about ideology in general. First, ideology is structured and selective. That is, it is organized into "persistent patterns of cognition, interpretation, and presentation, of selection, emphasis, and exclusion."[2] The public discussion of marihuana at any given time has not been a haphazard collection of observations and beliefs but has been organized around a coherent set of assumptions about the drug, its users, and the law.

Second, ideology is socially determined. That is, the specific ways in which ideology is structured or framed are in turn shaped by other social factors. The assumptions framing public discussion of marihuana have been the products of a complex set of factors: the specific set of organized actors struggling to shape drug control policy, the social background of the users of the drug, and broader social conflicts.

Third, ideology places certain tacit limits on how issues are discussed and what policy alternatives appear plausible and appropriate. It thus defines a political terrain and channels political action and social policy. The ideological framework within which marihuana has been discussed at any given time has constrained the arguments that could be raised effectively and the policies that could be forwarded plausibly. In particular, marihuana law reform resulted in part from radical changes in typical perceptions of users and in the kinds of arguments that were made about the law.

Fourth, ideology, therefore, is not a mere mask that hides the real social forces at work in a situation and must be ripped away to see what is "really" happening. It is an integral part of those forces. Explaining ideas sociologically does not mean explaining them away, or debunking them, but rather understanding their real causes and real effects. Marihuana ideology has been a crucial mediating link between marihuana law and the wider social forces that shaped the law. Changes in the organized groups seeking to shape drug control policy, in the social location of use, and in the broader conflicts within which use has been embedded have caused changes in the terms in which marihuana has been discussed. These changes in turn have affected the content of marihuana laws.

In the following chapters, we shall not only critically refine existing explanations of marihuana laws and how they have changed, but we shall also focus scholarly attention squarely on marihuana ideology, on how the public discussion of marihuana has been framed. In particular, we shall systematically compare public discussion of marihuana in two phases of the drug's history—before and after the mid-1960s.

To explore these issues, we shall rely on a systematic sample of magazine articles drawn from the *Readers' Guide to Periodical Literature* to provide a representative picture of public discussion of marihuana as it has developed since the 1890s. This data will be put to two uses. On one level, the relative frequency of articles on marihuana in the *Readers' Guide* will allow us to determine the changing importance of the marihuana issue over the years, a matter that is interesting in itself and central for evaluating some of the marihuana hypotheses. The results of this "magnitude study" are reported in chapter 3. On another level, a content analysis of the *Readers' Guide* articles will help us to identify the changing images of the drug and its users. Each article (N = 106) in this "content study" has been examined for what, if anything, it has to say about how dangerous marihuana is, whether or not moderate (limited, safe) use is possible, what specific dangers marihuana presents, and who the typical users are. The results, which will be drawn upon throughout the following chapters, will allow us both to evaluate the various marihuana hypotheses and to trace the changing image of the drug. Above all, the content study will help us to compare rigorously public discussion of marihuana before and after the mid-1960s. The data from the magnitude and content studies will be supplemented by a variety of other primary materials, especially congressional hearings, the reports of national commissions and narcotics officials, and newspaper articles.[3]

The remainder of this chapter examines certain basic concepts that inform the scholarly literature on drugs and underlie our own discussion. Chapter 2 provides more historical and theoretical groundwork by summarizing the important features of marihuana history in the United States and then presenting the four marihuana hypotheses to which we have alluded. Chapters 3 through 5 examine marihuana in the period prior to the mid-1960s: Chapter 3 presents an overview of the magnitude and content of public discussion of marihuana over some six-and-a-half decades; chapter 4 traces the origins of the Marihuana Tax Act and the ideological consensus that surrounded it; and chapter 5 looks at continuities and changes in that consensus in the 1940s, 1950s, and early 1960s. Chapters 6 and 7 examine the path of marihuana law reform in the late 1960s and early 1970s and the concomitant transformation of marihuana from "killer weed" to "drop-out drug." Chapter 8 summarizes our various arguments and makes some general points about the role of ideas in society and history.

GUIDING CONCEPTS

Any study of marihuana must start from the broader scholarly literature on drug controls that has mushroomed in the last two decades. The growth of this literature is in itself an interesting phenomenon that is closely related to the marihuana story. Until the early 1960s, there was little serious historical inquiry into why some drugs are illegal and others are not or why some drugs are regarded as evil and others as beneficent—the kind of questions that we readily pose about marihuana today. Such issues simply were not regarded as problematic. It was taken for granted that some drugs were inherently dangerous and hence necessarily subject to social stigma and legal controls. There seemed to be no need to pose deeper historical, social, and political questions.

To be sure, there were some exceptions. In the late nineteenth century, Edward Forbes Robinson noted a political dimension to the history of coffee in England: The coffee houses that proliferated after 1650 were often associated with Puritanism and sometimes became centers of opposition to the Stuarts. As a result, in 1675, Charles II attempted unsuccessfully to have them closed. Louis Lewin in his 1924 classic *Phantastica* argued that the Spanish effort in the mid-1500s to ban coca chewing among their Incan slaves in the Americas followed from a complex of "political, economic, social, and religious reasons." The debate over temperance and Prohibition in the United States generated such serious studies as Peter Odegard's account of the Anti-Saloon League, the classic work on the prototypical political pressure group.[4] The historical research of Alfred Lindesmith and Rufus King on opiate controls in the United States and Great Britain also goes back several decades.

These examples, however distinguished some of them are, are few and far between. They certainly do not constitute a research

tradition with shared assumptions and a coherent line of development. Until recently, moreover, work consisted primarily of de-
scriptive historical accounts of drug controls that rarely sought
theoretical explanations. Robinson's work, for example, is primarily
a straightforward history of the spread of coffee use from Abyssinia
to the Islamic world and ultimately to Europe. Lewin's work is a
compendium of the cross-cultural array of psychoactive drug use.
Similarly, Charles Terry and Mildred Pellens compiled a vast amount
of materials on the history of opium in their classic 1928 volume,
The Opium Problem, which is still the starting point for any serious
study of the topic.[5] They do not, however, develop any theories of
opium and opiate control. They are not primarily interested in
explaining why California outlawed opium smoking in 1881 or
why opiates came under federal control in the 1914 Harrison Act.

A systematic, theoretically informed tradition of work concerned
precisely with the "political, economic, social, and religious reasons" for drug controls has arisen only in the last twenty years as a
result of both a wider reorientation in the study of deviance as a
whole and the explosive political conflict over drug controls in the
United States and other Western countries. Both these factors
rendered drug controls a problematic issue.

Prior to the 1960s, the study of deviance was almost exclusively
concerned with behavior questions: Why are some individuals more
likely than others to commit deviant acts? Why do some social
groups have higher deviance rates than others? While much attention was given to the causes of deviant behavior, little time was
spent on the societal reaction to that behavior. With the codification
of labelling theory in the early 1960s and the subsequent development of various radical, critical, conflict, and phenomenological
theories of deviance, however, attention has turned to labelling
questions: How and why do certain acts and actors become defined
as deviant and treated accordingly? What are the consequences of
this labelling? A growing concern with the historical and social
roots of drug controls has been simply one instance of this broader
shift of intellectual focus.

In the 1960s, laws controlling the use of marihuana and other
so-called narcotics (including heroin and cocaine) were widely
attacked. Powerful movements emerged to redefine drug use as a
public health problem, not a law enforcement problem, or to remove the deviant label altogether. Once drug controls became

politically contentious, they were bound to become intellectually problematic as well. Once the inevitability and the legitimacy of drug controls were widely challenged, questions about their social and historical roots were quick to follow.[6]

Central to the recently developed drug control literature are three guiding concepts that will prove useful in our study of marihuana. These are "entrepreneurship," "social locus," and "symbolic politics." They are not the only significant ideas in work on drug controls, but they figure prominently, either individually or in various combinations, in most studies. We can examine them one by one in the works of Howard Becker, Troy Duster, and Joseph Gusfield, respectively.[7] Although these writers have had a significant impact on the field, their studies should be viewed primarily as ideal types, not as prototypes. They embody in particularly clear, unalloyed form ideas that other works leave implicit or combine together. In each case, we will be concerned not with the immediate empirical validity of the author's work but with the wider potential of his analytic framework.

Entrepreneurship

One way of understanding drug controls is to study the formal processes through which they were created. That is, we can pay attention to who took the initiative to procure a particular drug law and how and why they did so. This is the general approach underlying Becker's concept of "moral entrepreneurship."

Moral rules, Becker reminds us, are not automatically created and enforced. Although we often colloquially refer to "society" per se as the force that labels and punishes deviance, the agency is rarely so impersonal or amorphous. Rule creation and rule enforcement require "moral enterprise," the specific effort by a formally constituted agent to transform established social values into specific rules and then to see to it that these rules are applied. Such an agent is a "moral entrepreneur."

Deviance—in the sense I have been using it, of publicly labeled wrongdoing—is always the result of enterprise. Before any act can be viewed as deviant, and before any class of people can be labeled and treated as outsiders for committing the act, someone must have made the rule which defines the act as deviant. Rules are not made automatically.[8]

To procure a new moral rule, the moral entrepreneur must go through a characteristic process: The agent must make public the relevant area of wrongdoing, enlist the support of other interested organizations, develop a favorable public attitude toward the new rule through use of the media, and resolve possible conflicts of interests and values.[9] Becker traces this process in the case of the U.S. Federal Bureau of Narcotics and the Marihuana Tax Act, which we shall say much more about later.

Becker's analysis thus focuses on who makes the rules and how they make them. He is less concerned with the question of why, the motives and interests of the moral entrepreneur. Contrary to the almost universal interpretation of his work, although he identifies the "crusading reformer" who seeks to eradicate "evil" as a major variety of moral entrepreneur, he never says that all moral entrepreneurs are motivated by moral concerns. Indeed he explicitly argues that the entrepreneurial motive or interest may vary and does not give the matter a central place in his analysis.[10]

To adapt the concept of entrepreneurship as a general analytic tool, we must make several corrections to Becker's analysis. First, just as rules are not automatically created, so individuals and groups do not automatically become moral entrepreneurs. They may be moral entrepreneurs only at some times and with regard to some issues. As we shall see, for example, the Federal Bureau of Narcotics was morally enterprising with regard to marihuana in 1937 but not in 1932; it provided the enterprise to tighten controls over marihuana and heroin in the 1950s but refused to play the same role with barbiturates. Moral entrepreneurship also must be explained, and to do so, we must address the question of motives and interests that Becker skirts. What motivates a particular group to seek the creation of a particular rule at a particular time?

Second, the world of enterprise is seldom as sparsely populated as Becker seems to imply. There is rarely just one moral entrepreneur, one organized force seeking a moral rule. There are usually several moral entrepreneurs seeking different rules on the same issue and a few "immoral entrepreneurs," who attempt to oppose or rescind a rule. In the case of America's original narcotics legislation, the Harrison Act of 1914, drug manufacturers and states's rights interests opposed all federal controls; medical and pharmacist associations supported professional controls; and law enforcement officials in the Treasury Department ultimately pushed for total criminalization. Similarly variegated groups of entrepreneurs attempted to influence international alcohol controls in the late 1800s and early 1900s.[11] An adequate entrepreneurial analysis, therefore, must recognize the plurality of organizations and organized interests that may shape a moral rule and must identify their various conflicts and alliances.

Third, in such a complicated world the process of rule creation must be far more complex than Becker pictures it. The would-be moral entrepreneur must not only publicize issues, enlist support, and cultivate public opinion but also fight other enterprising groups. Power thus becomes an issue in a way that Becker's model does not anticipate. An entrepreneurial analysis, therefore, must identify and explain the power differentials among the various groups involved in the rule-creation process.

Making the adjustments suggested in the three foregoing criticisms of Becker yields a more sophisticated entrepreneurial model of drug controls, which views the creation of drug laws as the outcome of the interaction of various would-be moral entrepreneurs, each with its distinctive material and moral resources, interests, and ideology. The result is something akin to the general model for analyzing social problems presented by Robert Ross and Graham L. Staines.[12]

This model is still incomplete, however, and this leads to our fourth and final criticism of Becker's analysis. An entrepreneurial analysis, even a very sophisticated one, looks exclusively at the explicit efforts of formally organized groups to shape drug laws. It pays no attention to the wider social context in which specific moral enterprising occurs and thus often ignores broader structural determinants. Within this approach, society itself disappears. In fact, however, the political process of defining a drug problem and establishing drug laws does not occur in a vacuum. The moral enterprise of the Women's Christian Temperance Union against alcohol—one of Becker's two examples—developed out of the crisis of the middle classes in a rapidly changing capitalist society. The successful effort to outlaw opium smoking in California in 1881 arose from broader economic conflict between Anglo and Chinese laborers. The different entrepreneurial roles played by the medical profession in the development of narcotics control in the United States, Canada, and Great Britain resulted from cross-national differences in patterns of opiate use and the social status of the profession. In each case, the wider context of entrepreneurial action proved crucial.[13]

Fortified with these corrective insights, the concept of entrepreneurship can provide a viable basis for an analysis of drug controls that pays particular attention to the rule-creating actions of organizations and organized interest groups and to the role of power and interests therein.

Social Locus

The concept of "social locus" posits a relationship between the moral status of a particular kind of drug use and the social position of the groups identified as the primary users. The lower the social position of the user, the more likely that use will be regarded as deviant. As the social location of use changes, so does its moral status. Thus in contrast to the focus of entrepreneurship on who creates the rules, social locus turns our attention to who uses a drug.

The argument here is based on the assumption that the deviant label is "totalizing." Drawing on the work of Everett Hughes and Becker, Duster argues that most labelling or status attribution is partial: We view others as being a certain way only in a limited respect. The deviant label is different, however. Once we regard someone as deviant in one respect, we tend to generalize our judgment to the whole person. We believe that the deviant status is, in Duster's phrase, "thoroughly indicative of the person." Or, to use Hughes's language, deviance is a "master status-determining trait" that "tends to overpower, in most crucial situations, any other characteristic which runs counter to it." According to Duster's logic, then, labelling someone a "dope fiend" places a moral judgment not only on his drug use but also on his entire being. He is thoroughly "disreputable."[14]

Because the deviant label is totalizing and negative, a "status contradiction" develops anytime it is placed on the actions of someone whose other master statuses (for example, class or race) imply a general respectability. No such contradiction arises, however, if these other statuses imply disreputability. Thus, it is easier to label as deviant the actions characteristic of the lower classes and low-status racial groups than those of the upper and middle classes and of high-status racial groups. The moral status of a category of acts, therefore, may depend on the social position of those perceived as the typical perpetrators. As Duster puts it:

Certain classes of persons in any society are more susceptible to being charged with moral inferiority than other classes of persons. The behavior in which persons indulge is often less important than the social category from which they come. . . . When it is part of the public view that the predominant perpetrators of the act come from the moral center, the act cannot long remain "immoral" or deviant; it can become deviant again only under circumstances where the public conception is that the "morally susceptible" classes are those who are the primary indulgers.[15]

Duster cites the moral career of opiate use as an example. In the United States in the nineteenth and early twentieth centuries, when opiate (primarily morphine) users were predominantly upper- and middle-class (as well as middle-aged and female), opiate addiction was not regarded as deviant. It was seen as an unfortunate physical malady, but it was not taken as a sign that the addict was essentially morally depraved or psychologically unbalanced. In other words, it carried no stigma. With the ban on over-the-counter opiate sales embodied in the 1914 Harrison Act and the limitations on physician prescriptions imposed by subsequent judicial interpretations of the act, however, major changes occurred in the public perceptions of the opiate user's social position. Upper- and middle-class users faded from public view as they made clandestine, quasi-legal arrangements with their physicians; and users of a new kind became visible—lower-class persons who procured their drugs illegally or who resorted to the few freely prescribing "script" physicians or to the official narcotic clinics. The opiate user now appeared as an otherwise disreputable person, and the moral status of opiate addiction changed accordingly: It was now taken as a clear sign of psychopathology, immorality, or both.

The same conclusion, Duster adds, can be drawn from the history of alcohol in the United States. In the early 1900s, alcohol use was associated with the lower classes and thus was regarded as deviant. With the advent of Prohibition, which left no loopholes for the middle and upper classes, the illicit alcohol use of more respectable elements of society became publicly visible, "producing the conditions for a public reappraisal of the moral status of alcohol consumption."[16]

We can transform Duster's "social locus" analysis into a general conceptual tool if we are mindful of two caveats. First, Duster's social distinctions are often vague. While he refers to the "moral center," the "decent and respectable elements" of society, and to "unrespectable elements," it is unclear where the "line of respectability" is drawn and which social groups fit where. At some points, the "unrespectable elements" appear to include simply the criminal strata of society; at other points, the working class as well. Although some imprecision creeps into any set of social distinctions, an effective social locus concept requires a bit more clarity.

Second, we ought not to reduce the complexity of social position to the simple notion of status honor in the Weberian sense, of respectability and disrespectability. There are other features of social position that may affect how readily the acts of a group are labelled deviant. Some social groups may be more prone to deviant labelling because they lack the power to organize and to affect the process of morality creation. Power, in this sense, consists of many components of which status honor, or moral repute, is only one. Effective use of a social locus concept requires a more variegated notion of how a group's social position may influence the moral judgment placed on its action.

Symbolic Politics

The "symbolic politics" concept understands drug controls as symbolic counters in wider social conflicts. At times of social conflict or stress, the drug use of a socially subordinate group may become a symbol of the threat that this group poses to a relatively dominant social group or to the dominant social order. Legislation against drug use thus may become a way of reasserting the legitimacy of the existing social hierarchy and the hegemony of dominant social groups by symbolically condemning those groups that threaten that hierarchy and hegemony. Unlike entrepreneurship, which studies the rule makers, and social locus, which attends to the drug user, the concept of symbolic politics focuses on the wider structural conflicts between drug-using groups and legislation-seeking groups.

We can understand this notion by looking at Gusfield's analysis of the prohibitionist phase of the Temperance Movement in the United States. Gusfield distinguishes two kinds of politics—class politics and status politics:

In our usage class politics is political conflict over the allocation of material resources. Status politics is political conflict over the allocation of prestige.

In class politics . . . we have conflict between the material goals and aspirations of different social groups such as is found in the traditional right and left. In status politics the conflict arises from status aspirations and discontents.[17]

Class politics, in other words, seeks to procure state policies that provide direct material advantages to particular social groups, for example, protective tariffs, minimum wage laws, welfare legislation, subsidies for farmers. Status politics seeks policies that reflect and affirm the culture, lifestyle, and thus the status position of particular social groups. According to Gusfield, "moral reform" movements are one variety of status politics.

Issues of moral reform . . . are one way through which a cultural group acts to preserve, defend, or enhance the dominance and prestige of its own style of living within the total society.[18]

Even if not enforced, moral reform legislation stands as a symbolic affirmation of a particular group's morality and thus of their prestige: "The public support of one conception of morality at the expense of another enhances the prestige and self-esteem of the victors and degrades the culture of the losers."[19]

The movement to prohibit alcohol use, Gusfield continues, is the prime example of status politics in American history. In the late nineteenth century, the Temperance Movement turned from "assimilative reform," an attempt to reform individual drunkards, to "coercive reform," an effort to procure state and ultimately national legislation against the production and sale of alcohol. The new emphasis, Gusfield argues, reflected the effort of a predominantly Protestant, native-born, rural, old middle class to reassert its status position in the face of a rising urban, corporate capitalist, industrial society and a growing non-Protestant, immigrant working class. Prohibition was a symbolic assertion of the dominance of abstemious old middle-class norms concerning alcohol use and of the old middle-class society in general over more permissive alcohol norms and the new society and new classes that these norms symbolized.

Prohibition, in short, was a form of *symbolic action* taken by the old middle class in response to threats to its status from an emerging new society. Symbolism enters here on two levels. First, alcohol use was a symbol of the general threat that this emerging society posed to the old middle class: The conflict over alcohol stood for a wider conflict between two social worlds. Second, the impact of anti-alcohol legislation was symbolic: What mattered was not its enforcement but simply its existence as a public statement of morality.

Gusfield thus exemplifies the analysis of drug controls as symbolic politics—as symbolic action in the context of social conflict. Before this concept can be rendered generally useful, however, it must be freed from the notions of class and status politics with which Gusfield shackles it.

The distinction between class politics and status politics in itself is unsatisfactory as a way of conceptualizing the varieties of political conflict. It simply leaves out too much. Many political issues cannot be reduced to struggles over the allocation of either material resources or prestige. Consider the classic issues of nineteenth-century European politics—parliamentary democracy, capitalism, the relationship between church and state—or some of the major movements in American history—antislavery, populism, civil rights, feminism. None of these is class politics, status politics, or some simple combination of the two. They all involve controversy over some fundamental features of society, while both class politics and status politics refer to conflict over the distribution of valued things within a generally accepted societal framework.[20]

More importantly, not all symbolic politics is necessarily status politics. That is, social conflict of many kinds, not just status conflict, may give rise to symbolic political action. Patricia Morgan, for example, argues that California's 1881 law against opium smoking was a response to economic conflict between Anglo and Chinese workers.[21] Indeed, the social conflict in which Gusfield situates Prohibition in his work appears to be much more than a status conflict. It is a struggle between entirely divergent social worlds and thus has many components. Furthermore, if symbolic politics may be based in conflicts of various kinds, it may also affirm domination of various kinds—economic, political, and ideological, as well as status domination.[22] In short, the important idea from Gusfield for the study of drug controls is "symbolic action in the context of social conflict," not "status politics."

Entrepreneurship, social locus, and symbolic politics will all prove helpful to our discussion of marihuana laws and ideoloy. They underlie the marihuana hypotheses to be presented in the next chapter and provide the basis for understanding the transformation of marihuana from a "killer weed" to a "drop-out drug."

NOTES

1. Robert Goldman, "Dope Invades the Suburbs," *The Saturday Evening Post,* 4 April 1964, pp. 19-25; "Narcotics: Slum to Suburb," *Newsweek,* 22 February 1965, pp. 68A-68C; "Pot Problem," *Time,* 12 March 1965, p. 49; Jeremy Larner, "The College Drug Scene," *The Atlantic Monthly,* November 1965, pp. 127-130.

2. Todd Gitlin, *The Whole World Is Watching: Mass Media in the Making and Unmaking of the New Left* (Berkeley: University of California, 1980), p. 7.

3. See the Methodological Appendix for a detailed discussion of the research methods used in this study.

4. Edward Forbes Robinson, *The Early History of Coffee Houses in England* (London: Kegan Paul, 1893); Louis Lewin, *Phantastica* (New York: E. P. Dutton, 1964), pp. 75-76; and Peter Odegard, *Pressure Politics* (New York: Columbia University Press, 1928).

5. Charles Terry and Mildred Pellens, *The Opium Problem* (1928; reprint ed., Montclair, N.J.: Patterson, Smith, 1970).

6. For a more detailed discussion of the intellectual and political antecedents of drug control theory, see Jerome L. Himmelstein, "Drug Politics Theory: Analysis and Critique," *Journal of Drug Issues* 8 (1978):37-52.

7. Howard S. Becker, *Outsiders: Studies in the Sociology of Deviance* (New York: Free Press, 1963); Troy Duster, *The Legislation of Morality* (New York: Free Press, 1970); Joseph R. Gusfield, *Symbolic Crusade* (Urbana: University of Illinois, 1963).

8. Becker, *Outsiders,* p. 162.

9. Ibid., pp. 122, 132, 138-139.

10. Ibid., pp. 122, 138, 147-148.

11. David F. Musto, *The American Disease* (New Haven: Yale University, 1973); Lynn Pan, *Alcohol in Colonial Africa* (Helsinki: Finnish Foundation for Alcohol Studies, 1975).

12. Robert Ross and Graham L. Staines, "The Politics of Analyzing Social Problems," *Social Problems* 20 (1972):18-40.

13. Gusfield, *Symbolic Crusade;* Patricia A. Morgan, "The Legislation of Drug Laws," *Journal of Drug Issues* 8 (1978):53-62; Shirley J. Cook,

Variations in Response to Illegal Drug Use (Toronto: Alcoholism and Drug Addiction Research Foundation, 1970).

14. Everett C. Hughes, "Dilemmas and Contradictions of Status," *American Journal of Sociology* 50 (1945):353-359; Becker, *Outsiders,* pp. 32-34.

15. Duster, *Legislation of Morality,* p. 247.

16. Ibid., p. 248.

17. Gusfield, *Symbolic Crusade,* pp. 18, 17.

18. Ibid., p. 3.

19. Ibid., p. 5.

20. Gusfield effectively admits this limitation since he situates his concepts in American society, where, he argues, there has generally been a "consensus about fundamentals" (ibid., p. 2).

21. Morgan, "Legislation of Drug Laws."

22. Any discussion of symbolic politics should mention the seminal work of Murray Edelman. See Edelman, *The Symbolic Uses of Politics* (Urbana: University of Illinois, 1964) and *Politics as Symbolic Action* (Chicago: Markham, 1971).

FOUR HYPOTHESES IN SEARCH OF REALITY

Two issues have preoccupied those who have studied the history of marihuana in the United States: the origins of the federal anti-marihuana legislation in the 1930s and the widespread controversy over the drug that characterized the late 1960s and early 1970s and has not yet been wholly resolved. In each case, work has been guided by two specific hypotheses. The Marihuana Tax Act of 1937 has been explained as the result of the entrepreneurial activity of the Federal Bureau of Narcotics (FBN) or as a reflection of the grass-roots anti-Mexican sentiment arising from Anglo-Mexican conflict in the Southwest. We shall call the former notion the "Anslinger Hypothesis" after Harry Anslinger, the commissioner of the FBN from its creation in 1930 to his retirement in 1962, and the latter the "Mexican Hypothesis." Growing support for marihuana law reform in the last twelve years has been linked to the increase in use among the middle class, while the often strident opposition to such reform has been tied to marihuana's role as a symbol of the Counterculture. We shall dub these two assertions respectively the "Embourgeoisement Hypothesis" and the "Hippie Hypothesis." Before examining in detail what these hypotheses tell us and what evidence bears on each, let us first look briefly at the history of marihuana use and controls in the United States.

A BRIEF HISTORY OF MARIHUANA

The *Cannabis sativa* or hemp plant has been cultivated for its fiber, its seeds, and its leaves, flowering tops, and resin.[1] The fiber has been used in linen, canvas, and rope; the seeds in bird food and as the source of a fast-drying oil; and the leaves, flowering tops, and resin for a variety of religious, medicinal, and psychoactive purposes. Preparations of cannabis for this last set of uses have had a large number of names—marihuana (marijuana), hashish, kif, bhang, ganja, karas, pot, grass, and many others. We shall simply call them marihuana.

Although there is some controversy about exactly when marihuana was first used, its history extends well into antiquity. Chinese and Indian use may date as early as several millenia before Christ and certainly no later than 800 B.C. Its use in mid-Asia by the Scythians, Persians, and Assyrians occurred as early as 700 B.C., and it was established in the Islamic world by A.D. 1000. In subsequent centuries, it was spread by the Arabs to Africa and the Mediterranean. The practice of smoking has a later origin, arising only after the introduction of tobacco into the Old World in the sixteenth and seventeenth centuries.

While Europeans had cultivated cannabis for its fiber at least as early as the Renaissance, psychoactive use was introduced only in the nineteenth century when Napoleon's armies brought hashish back to France from Egypt. The drug, however, did not become popular beyond the small group of artists and writers (including Gautier, Hugo, Baudelaire, and Balzac) who made up the "Club des Haschischins."

Spanish and English settlers introduced the cannabis plant into the New World for fiber and seed in the sixteenth and seventeenth centuries, and it was a major crop in the United States through the nineteenth century. Cultivation fell off in the late 1800s as imported hemp fiber proved cheaper, but it left a legacy of hundreds of thousands of acres of wild marihuana, the eradication of which would become a major problem for U.S. law enforcement officials in the 1930s.

Cannabis extracts were used by physicians in the United States in the late nineteenth and early twentieth centuries to treat a number

of conditions including menstrual cramps, asthma, opiate withdrawal symptoms, cough, insomnia, lack of appetite, and convul-
sions. The *United States Pharmacopeia* listed marihuana as a
recognized medicine from 1850 through 1942. Effective use of the
drug, however, was always hampered by its insolubility in water,
slow action, variable potency, and the inconsistency of patient
response. With the introduction of new synthetic drugs in the 1900s,
it quickly fell into disuse.

Psychoactive use of cannabis was rare in the United States before
the twentieth century, beyond some experimental use of hashish
by the writers Fitzhugh Ludlow and Bayard Taylor. Marihuana
use did flourish, however, in Mexico and Central America in the
late nineteenth century, and Mexican laborers seeking agricultural
work brought the drug into the United States in the early 1900s.
Marihuana use was noted among Mexican populations in Texas
in the 1910s and eventually throughout the West and Southwest
and as far north as Chicago in the 1920s. The drug spread to poor
blacks in the 1920s, first in New Orleans and later throughout the
South and North. It was used by both black and white jazz musicians
by the 1930s and had spread to the beat culture of New York and
San Francisco and to some intellectual and artistic groups by the
1950s. Despite the lurid late-1930s propaganda, however, marihuana
use prior to the 1960s was neither large-scale nor prevalent among
adolescents.

Marihuana use in the United States increased dramatically in
the 1960s and spread particularly to middle-class youth. The changing
use patterns had their roots in the influx of adolescents into the
beat scene in the late 1950s and the growing public attention given
to experimentation with psychedelics in the early 1960s. The beat
and psychedelic worlds were relatively accessible to adolescents and
college youth, and the alienated stance of each to the dominant
society made marihuana use appear as a suitable symbol of youthful
rebellion. The first Gallup Poll on marihuana in 1969 showed that
4 percent of the American people had used the drug at least once.
By 1973, 12 percent had; by 1977, 24 percent. Prevalence rates
were particularly high among college students. According to the
Gallup Poll, 22 percent of all college students had tried marihuana
by 1969, and by 1974, over half had done so. The 1977 Gallup Poll
showed that although marihuana use had diffused widely through-

out the population, it remained most common among those under thirty and those with a college education.

The legal history of marihuana is quite distinct from that of heroin or cocaine. It was not included in the 1914 Harrison Act or the 1922 Narcotic Drug Import-Export Act, the original federal laws that controlled opium and coca derivatives. The first legal controls on marihuana use in the United States originated at the local level and with a few exceptions followed the diffusion of the drug. The city of El Paso passed the first ordinance to ban the sale and possession of the drug in 1914; and based on a complaint from that city, importation of marihuana for nonmedical purposes was banned by the federal government in the next year under the provisions of the 1906 Food and Drug Act. By 1933, thirty-three states— twenty west of the Mississippi—had legislation against nonmedical distribution of marihuana. Between 1933 and 1940, nearly all the states adopted the Uniform Narcotic Drugs Act and usually with a provision against marihuana.

After the inclusion of marihuana in the Food and Drug Act in 1915, nothing was done about marihuana on the federal level until 1929, when the act establishing two "narcotics farms" for treating "addicts" classified "Indian Hemp" for the first time as a "narcotic." In 1934, the Federal Bureau of Narcotics began to publicize the alleged dangers of marihuana use to convince states to pass the Uniform Narcotic Drugs Act. Subsequently, the bureau turned its attention to the federal level, where it convinced Congress to pass the Marihuana Tax Act, which made the sale and use of marihuana federal offenses. Penalties for these offenses were increased and standardized with those for other narcotics in the 1951 Boggs Act and the 1956 Narcotics Control Act, which were copied by most of the states. In contrast, the 1960s and 1970s witnessed significant reductions and in some cases removal of criminal penalties for marihuana use, a matter that we shall discuss in detail in chapter 6.

Responsibility for the enforcement of federal narcotics laws has moved from agency to agency over the years. Prior to 1930, the 1914 Harrison Act (controlling the domestic production and sale of narcotics) was policed first by the Internal Revenue Service and then by the Prohibition Bureau, while the 1922 Narcotic Drugs Import-Export Act was the province of the Federal Narcotics Control Board. In 1930, with Prohibition on the skids, these two narcotics control functions were joined in the Federal Bureau of Narcotics, a newly created agency in the Department of Treasury. The FBN maintained its aegis over narcotics until the mid-1960s, when pursuant to the recommendation of the President's 1963 Advisory Commission on Narcotic and Drug Abuse, President Lyndon Johnson combined all control of illicit drug traffic in the Justice Department's Bureau of Narcotics and Dangerous Drugs and all control of licit production in the Food and Drug Administration. In 1973, President Richard Nixon created the Drug Enforcement Agency as the overseer of illicit drug control.

THE MARIHUANA TAX ACT OF 1937

Everyone who has studied the Marihuana Tax Act of 1937 acknowledges the role of the Federal Bureau of Narcotics in its passage. The matter is not controversial. The important question is what kind of role did it play? The answer to this question distinguishes the Anslinger Hypothesis from the Mexican Hypothesis. The Anslinger Hypothesis argues that the FBN, acting on its own initiative, turned marihuana use into a public issue and procured passage of the Marihuana Tax Act. The Mexican Hypothesis argues that the marihuana issue was rooted in anti-Mexican sentiment in the West and Southwest and that the Marihuana Tax Act was the direct or indirect result of racially motivated pressure from that part of the country. In this view, rather than creating an issue, the bureau merely capitalized on already existing concern; rather than seeking legislation on its own initiative, it reacted to local pressure.

The Anslinger Hypothesis dates at least back to Howard Becker's research in the early 1950s and for a long time dominated the field. Although Alfred Lindesmith and others suggested in the 1960s that disapproval of marihuana use was based on its association with the "lower classes," serious consideration of the Mexican Hypothesis developed only in the work of David Musto and John Helmer in the early 1970s.[2]

To facilitate discussion and comparison of these two hypotheses, let us further specify what is at issue. In the early 1930s, as definitive marihuana historians Richard Bonnie and Charles Whitebread II have shown, the Federal Bureau of Narcotics steadfastly denied that marihuana use was a problem and argued strongly against any federal legislation.[3] By 1935, however, the bureau was decrying the "marihuana menace" as part of its effort to procure state adoption of the Uniform Narcotic Drugs Act, and by 1936 it was making plans to seek a national law. Any explanation of the bureau's behavior must ultimately explain why this reversal occurred when it did.

The Anslinger Hypothesis

The Anslinger Hypothesis is an application of the notion of entrepreneurship, and its classic formulation comes from Becker: "The Treasury Department's Bureau of Narcotics furnished most of the enterprise that produced the Marihuana Tax Act." Central to the history of this act, Becker argues, is "the story of an entrepreneur whose initiative and enterprise overcame public apathy and indifference."[4]

To support his assertion, Becker notes the FBN's verbal support for marihuana legislation in its annual reports in the mid-1930s and its predominant role during the congressional hearings. He also points out that those magazine articles at the time that called attention to the marihuana problem often bore the mark of the bureau's influence: Of the seventeen articles indexed in *The Readers' Guide to Periodical Literature* from July 1937 to June 1939, ten explicitly acknowledged its help or simply cited facts from its publications and testimony; others repeated marihuana "atrocity stories" that originated with the bureau.

Becker does not concern himself, however, with the FBN's motives in seeking antimarihuana legislation. He is more concerned with how and who than with why. Indeed he explicitly sidesteps the issue.

While it is, of course, difficult to know what the motives of Bureau officials were, we need assume no more than that they perceived an area of wrongdoing that properly belonged in their jurisdiction and moved to put it there. The personal interest they satisfied in pressing for marihuana legislation was one common to many officials: the interest in successfully accomplishing the task one has been assigned and in acquiring the best tools with which to accomplish it.[5]

In other words, the issue of motivation is not problematic, and thus we can assume the simplest explanation. Contrary to some interpretations, Becker never refers to the bureau as a "moral crusader" or a "crusading reformer," nor does he suggest that the bureau sought antimarihuana legislation for moralistic reasons. He simply does not address the issue of motivation.

Many subsequent writers, either following Becker's lead or working independently, have adopted the Anslinger Hypothesis.

[The Marihuana Tax Act] was the result of a publicity campaign staged by the Federal Bureau of Narcotics under Mr. Anslinger's direction and leadership.[6]

The Federal Bureau of Narcotics had created a villainous *bete noir* out of whole cloth.[7]

The 1937 Tax Act was the culmination of a series of efforts on the part of the Federal Bureau of Narcotics to generate antimarihuana legislation.[8]

In these and similar works attention is squarely on the bureau's actions.[9] These authors, however, never really question the nature of the FBN's role or justify their exclusive focus on the bureau. They simply assume that the bureau acted on its own initiative rather than being pushed and that it created the marihuana issue rather than adopting it. They rarely critically examine these assumptions or present data relevant to their validity.

The proponents of the Anslinger Hypothesis also hardly ever attempt to explain *why* the bureau acted as and when it did. They generally follow Becker, contenting themselves with describing what the bureau did. Those who offer explanations often do so in an offhand way. Joel Fort suggests that the FBN was trying to steal some of the publicity lavished on the Federal Bureau of Investigation, and Erich Goode describes the FBN as an "ideological imperialist" that desired to foist its views of right and wrong on the world.[10] Neither goes into detail or considers why the bureau sought a national law in 1936 but not a few years before.

An exception is Donald Dickson, who systematically argues that a need for "bureaucratic survival and growth," not a desire to legislate morality, was the primary factor in the bureau's decision to seek a national antimarihuana law.[11] He points out that 1936 was a good year for the bureau as a moral crusader but a bad year for it as a bureaucracy. Virtually every state had enacted a law against marihuana, but the bureau's budgetary appropriation was the lowest in a decade. Under these circumstances, the bureau began to push for a national marihuana law so that it could use its increased scope of operations as a basis for future demands for increased funding.

Although Dickson's argument is plausible, it runs into several problems. There is no evidence that the bureau used the Marihuana Tax Act in any systematic way to argue for subsequent budgetary increases, and as Dickson notes, no major increases were forthcoming. Subsequent research on the bureau's deliberations in 1935 and 1936, moreover, does not show that a desire to increase appropriations entered into the bureau's decision to seek a national law.[12] Finally, as we shall see, the bureau generally did not attempt to survive by expanding but by avoiding expansion and its attendant dangers of overcommitment and conflict with other vested interests.

The Anslinger Hypothesis, in short, remains primarily a description of the FBN's actions; it offers no convincing explanations. Its assumptions, moreover, remain unexamined by most of its proponents. Building upon the work of Bonnie and Whitebread and Patricia Morgan, we shall show that the bureau's motives were far different from those assumed by the Anslinger Hypothesis.[13] Far from being an aggrandizing bureaucracy, a rapacious moral crusader, or a publicity hound, the FBN was a rather diffident agency that sought to preserve its power by strictly limiting the affairs under its control. Constrained by low Depression budgetary appropriations and chastened by the experience of Prohibition, the bureau pushed for a governmental division of labor in which it made general drug control policy, and the states did most of the day-to-day enforcement. To this end, it attempted to get the states to adopt the Uniform Narcotic Drugs Act and first evoked the "marihuana menace" as part of this effort. Its subsequent support for federal legislation appears to be an unintended consequence of this earlier activity.

The Mexican Hypothesis

The Mexican Hypothesis generally follows the notion of symbolic politics, and its first serious proponent, David Musto, acknowledges the influence of Gusfield. Musto's general analysis of American narcotics controls runs as follows:

The most passionate support for legal prohibition of narcotics has been associated with fear of a given drug's effect on a specific minority. . . .

In each instance, use of a particular drug was attributed to an identifiable and threatening minority group. The occasion for legal prohibition of drugs for non-medical purposes appears to come at a time of social crisis between the drug-linked group and the rest of American society.[14]

"The attack on marihuana," Musto argues, "occurred in the 1930s when Chicanos became a distinct and visible unemployed minority."[15] The advent of the Depression made Mexican laborers who had immigrated to the United States in the previous decades an "unwelcome surplus" and heightened anti-Mexican sentiment in the Southwest. The anti-Mexican sentiment created an "intense" fear of marihuana, which was associated with Mexicans, and local officials pressured the federal government for an antimarihuana law. This pressure, Musto concludes, "could well have been sufficient to induce" the bureau to come up with an appropriate piece of legislation. He cites as evidence Anslinger's own claim that he acted only in response to grass-roots agitation.[16]

John Helmer makes a similar argument but goes into more detail and adds some original ramifications.[17] He locates the economic conflict in which antimarihuana sentiment thrived in California's urban areas, where the growing mass of unemployed Mexicans during the Depression were perceived as a welfare and crime problem and where a movement to deport surplus Mexican laborers developed. In this context, jailing Mexicans on marihuana charges became part of the general attempt to reduce the labor surplus, and an antimarihuana ideology became one way of unifying and giving legitimacy to the anti-Mexican sentiments of various social groups. In turn, the concern about marihuana led to "growing political pressure from the Southwest to put a federal ban of marijuana on the books and federal agents in the field." It also generated an "ideology of marijuana" that "grew independently of the original concern."[18]

Musto's and Helmer's arguments are plausible. There were, after all, intense anti-Mexican feelings in California in the early 1930s, and marihuana was identified as a drug used by Mexicans. They lack empirical support, however, at crucial points. Musto never shows that fear of marihuana was "intense" at the time, and Helmer does not document either a substantial rise in marihuana arrests in the 1930s or the role of an antimarihuana ideology in forging a broad coalition of anti-Mexican forces. As we shall see in chapter 3, concern about marihuana in California in the 1930s was almost nonexistent.[19]

Similarly, neither Musto nor Helmer provides much direct evidence of local political pressure on the federal government. In fact, they cite less than a handful of letters—two from Louisiana state officials to the surgeon general and the Prohibition commissioner in 1920; one from a U.S. marshal in Oklahoma to Anslinger in 1934; and one from a Colorado newspaper editor to Anslinger in 1936. Bonnie and Whitebread report perhaps another seven or eight expressions of concern and requests for national legislation between 1915 and 1937, but we are still left with but a dozen examples of pressure spread over twenty years. Some of these, moreover, do not come from the West, and most do not explicitly mention Mexicans.[20] Above all, there appears to have been no great increase in pressure just prior to the bureau's policy shift in 1935.

The pressure argument rests simply on Commissioner Anslinger's own account that the bureau was moved to act in 1935 by urgent requests from local officials. This, however, is not enough to make the case. As Bonnie and Whitebread and others have shown, Anslinger consistently exaggerated the magnitude of public concern over marihuana use at the time, and he may have continued to do so in retrospect. The bureau had an interest in portraying its request for a national law as a response to popular clamor, rather than as its own idiosyncratic decision.

The Mexican Hypothesis has identified an important relationship but has misconstrued its nature. The crucial link between Mexicans and federal marihuana policy was not locally based political pressure from the Southwest but a specific image of marihuana that emerged from the context of marihuana use by Mexicans and was used to justify antimarihuana legislation. Because Mexican laborers and other lower-class groups were identified as typical marihuana users, the drug was believed to cause the kinds of antisocial behavior associated with these groups, especially violent crime. This led to a particular image of marihuana as a "killer weed," which then was used to justify both the Uniform Narcotic Drug Act and the Marihuana Tax Act. We shall show how this image of marihuana developed in the Southwest and in New Orleans in the 1910s and 1920s, found its way into the federal bureaucracy in the 1930s, and ultimately framed public discussion of the drug until the 1960s.

Since the proponents of the Anslinger Hypothesis have not developed an effective theory of *why* the bureau acted as and when it did and the advocates of the Mexican Hypothesis have failed to show that local pressure pushed the bureau into seeking a national law, the basic questions about the Marihuana Tax Act posed earlier remain unanswered. Any effort to improve upon either approach should start with the realization that although the Mexican Hypothesis was developed as a rebuttal to the Anslinger Hypothesis, the intellectual impulses underlying the two are not necessarily contradictory. A complete understanding of the Marihuana Tax Act requires attention to both the bureau's actions and the social context in which it acted. What is needed is a synthesis of the two approaches that looks at the preexisting concern and beliefs about marihuana, the bureau's actions, and the connection between the two. In examining the origins of the Marihuana Tax Act and the genesis of the "killer weed" image, we shall construct such a synthesis.

THE GREAT MARIHUANA CONTROVERSY

The historical closeness of the great marihuana controversy of the 1960s and 1970s has often discouraged theoretical analysis. The major assessments of the period often have appeared too obvious, too commonsensical to require extended commentary or elaboration. Accordingly, the literature on the topic is limited. Neither the Embourgeoisement Hypothesis nor the Hippie Hypothesis has attracted detailed study, and this is the major problem with each hypothesis.

The Embourgeoisement Hypothesis

The Embourgeoisement Hypothesis is a fairly straightforward application of the social locus concept. It argues that the large-scale spread of marihuana use to middle-class youth in the 1960s led to a reevaluation of the drug's dangers and to pressure for marihuana law reform. The wholly negative image of marihuana and the draconian penalties for use that had been acceptable when users were socially marginal gave way once use shifted to the middle class.[21]

Thus stated, the Embourgeoisement Hypothesis has become such a commonplace of reflection on the late 1960s and early 1970s that little attention has been given to how it was accomplished. How exactly did a change in the social background of marihuana users influence perceptions of the drug's dangers and laws concerning its use? What were the mediating links? The most common answer to these questions in sociological and historical literature argues that the secret to the embourgeoisement of marihuana lay in self-interested policymakers and politically mobilized users. As marihuana use increased among middle-class youth in the late 1960s and as arrests for use skyrocketed, effective pressure for law reform came from powerful, influential parents, especially the policymakers themselves, who had a direct interest in preventing their children from being stigmatized as criminals. At the same time, this increase in middle-class marihuana use turned the users themselves into a political force capable of influencing public discussion of the drug and capable of procuring marihuana law reform through both diffuse pressure and special lobbies like the National Organization for the Reform of Marihuana Laws.

This answer may be termed "instrumental" because it focuses primarily on the political process through which individual and social actors rationally and consciously shaped public discussion of the marihuana issue. It seeks to find out how changes in the users' social background influenced social policy by looking at who was active in shaping that policy. There is much truth to this answer, and we shall expand upon it in the coming pages. At the same time, however, we shall develop a second answer (also present in the literature, but distinctly underdeveloped) and in the process point out the limits of the first. To be sure, self-interested policymakers and politically mobilized users were important, but they did not operate in a vacuum. The public discussion of marihuana and marihuana law always has occurred within an ideological framework, a tacit set of assumptions that shapes how the drug and drug laws are discussed and what political alternatives appear plausible and appropriate. The dynamic of interests and pressure groups shapes this framework to an extent, but it is also constrained by it. The ideological framework demarcates a political terrain; changes in the framework can alter this terrain. Thus, it is not enough to ask *who* effected marihuana law reform; we must also know something about the framework within which they worked.

The increase in middle-class marihuana use brought about marihuana law reform not only by shaping interests and pressure groups but also by directly altering the issues and arguments that could be raised plausibly about the drug and the law. In other words, it changed the way in which the public discussion of marihuana was framed. This new framework was more receptive to the notion that marihuana use was not so dangerous, and it rendered support for marihuana law reform more plausible. In our discussion of marihuana in the late 1960s and early 1970s, we shall examine the complex ways in which this ideological framework changed and the differences these changes made.

The Hippie Hypothesis

The Hippie Hypothesis is another application of the symbolic politics concept, and Gusfield's influence again is directly evident.[22] It argues that marihuana became associated with the political and cultural rebellion of its youthful users—what was known as the Counterculture—in the late 1960s. As the National Commission on Marihuana and Drug Abuse noted in 1972: "Few of us have not seen or heard of marihuana being used *en masse* at rock concerts, political demonstrations and gatherings of campus activists."[23] As a result, marihuana became a symbol for both adults and youth of youthful rebellion and intergenerational conflict. Disapproval of marihuana use came to reflect not what the drug did, but what it represented. As John Kaplan, the main proponent of this hypothesis, put it in 1970:

Today a great part of the objection to marihuana use is not based upon any effect of the drug, but rather upon the entire life-style that many associate with it. The public mind often conceives of the marijuana-user as a long-haired hippie, and even those sophisticated enough to realize the oversimplicity of this view often associate marijuana use with a life-style and a set of values very different from their own.[24]

Kaplan identified some of these values as hedonism, political radicalism, distrust of authority, and permissiveness.

In this context, condemning marihuana use became a symbolic way of condemning the Counterculture, and support for criminal penalties against the drug became a symbolic way of asserting the legitimacy of the dominant culture. Similarly, approval of marihuana and opposition to the existing laws were a symbolic approval of the Counterculture and condemnation of the dominant culture:

> If marijuana is legalized, it will be a symbolic victory for the youthful adherents of the experiential counter-culture. Keeping marijuana within the criminal law, on the other hand, will be an 'act of ceremonial deference' toward present middle class standards, as Prohibition was for the old middle class of the 1920s.[25]

Although the Hippie Hypothesis is quite plausible, it distinguishes more sharply between the effects of a drug and what it symbolizes than actual public discussion did. As we shall discover, most objections to marihuana were not explicitly based on what the drug symbolized but rather on its alleged effects. If the symbolic content of marihuana dominated public discussion, it did so in a less direct, less explicit way, not by preempting the discussion of effects but by shaping that discussion. We shall argue that the emergence of marihuana as a symbol of the youthful Counterculture was partly responsible for a shift in the effects imputed to marihuana from violence to passivity. The symbolic content of marihuana, in other words, intruded into public discussion in more complex ways than imagined by the Hippie Hypothesis.

The Anslinger, Mexican, Embourgeoisement, and Hippie hypotheses lay out the issues around which our consideration of the history of marihuana in the next five chapters will be organized. We shall combine an evaluation of these issues with an examination of the changing terms in which marihuana, its users, and the law were publicly discussed.

NOTES

1. The following account of marihuana history draws upon these works: Richard H. Blum and associates, *Utopiates* (New York: Atherton Press, 1964) and *Society and Drugs* (San Francisco: Jossey-Bass, 1969); Richard J. Bonnie and Charles Whitebread II, *The Marihuana Conviction* (Charlottesville: University of Virginia Press, 1974); Edward M. Brecher et al., *Licit and Illicit Drugs* (Boston: Little, Brown, 1972); Henry Brill, "Recurrent Patterns in the History of Drug Dependence and Some Interpretations," in *Drugs and Youth: Proceedings of the Rutgers Symposium on Drug Abuse,* ed. J. R. Wittenborn et al. (Springfield, Ill.: Charles Thomas, 1969), pp.

8-25; William A. Emboden, Jr., "Ritual Use of Cannabis Sativa: A Histori-
cal Ethnographic Survey," in *The Flesh of the Gods,* ed. Peter Furst (New
York: Praeger, 1972), pp. 214-236; Joel Fort, "Giver of Delight or Liberator
of Sin: Drug Use and 'Addiction' in Asia," *Bulletin on Narcotics* 17, no. 3
(1965):1-11 and 17, no. 4 (1965):13-19; Louis Lewin, *Phantastica* (New
York: E. P. Dutton, 1965); Ned Polsky, *Hustlers, Beats, and Others*
(Garden City, N.Y.: Doubleday, 1969), pp. 144-182; Richard E. Schultes,
"Man and Marihuana," *Natural History* 82 (August 1973):58-63; Soloman
M. Snyder, "What We Have Forgotten About Pot," *New York Times
Magazine,* 13 December 1970, pp. 26-27; Robert P. Walton, *Marihuana:
America's New Drug Problem* (Philadelphia: J. B. Lippincott, 1938). All
Gallup Poll data are courtesy of the American Institute of Public Opinion.
    2. Howard S. Becker, *Outsiders: Studies in the Sociology of Deviance*
(New York: Free Press, 1963); Alfred J. Lindesmith, *The Addict and the
Law* (New York: Random House, 1965); David Solomon, ed., *The Mari-
huana Papers* (New York: New American Library, 1966); Joel Fort, *The
Pleasure-Seekers* (New York: Grove Press, 1969); Shirley J. Cook, *Varia-
tions in Response to Illegal Drug Use* (Toronto: Alcoholism and Drug
Addiction Research Foundation, 1970); David F. Musto, *The American
Disease* (New Haven: Yale University Press, 1973) and "The Marihuana
Tax Act of 1937," *Archives of General Psychiatry* 26 (1972):101-108;
John Helmer, *Drugs and Minority Oppression* (New York: Seabury Press,
1975); John Helmer and Thomas Vietorisz, *Drug Use, the Labor Market
and Class Conflict* (Washington, D.C.: Drug Abuse Council, 1974).
    3. Bonnie and Whitebread, *Marihuana Conviction.*
    4. Becker, *Outsiders,* pp. 138, 135.
    5. Ibid., p. 138.
    6. Lindesmith, *Addict and Law,* p. 226.
    7. Solomon, *Marihuana Papers,* p. xvi.
    8. Lester Grinspoon, *Marihuana Reconsidered* (New York: Bantam,
1971), p. 22.
    9. Jerry Mandel, "Hashish, Assassins, and the Love of God," *Issues in
Criminology* 2 (1966):149-156; Joseph S. Oteri and Harvey A. Silvergate,
"In the Marketplace of Free Ideas: A Look at the Passage of the Marihuana
Tax Act," in *Marihuana: Myths and Realities,* ed J. L. Simmons (North
Hollywood, Calif.: Brandon House, 1967), pp. 136-162; Donald T. Dickson,
"Bureaucracy and Morality," *Social Problems* 16 (1968):143-156; Jerome H.
Skolnick, "Coercion to Virtue: The Enforcement of Morals," *Southern
California Law Review* 41 (1968):588-641; Fort, *Pleasure-Seekers;* Roger
Smith, "U.S. Marihuana Legislation and the Creation of a Social Problem,"
in *The New Social Drug,* ed. David Smith (Englewood Cliffs, N.J.: Prentice-
Hall, 1970), pp. 105-117; Brecher, *Drugs;* Erich Goode, *Drugs in American*

Society (New York: Knopf, 1972); Rufus King, *The Drug Hang-up* (Springfield, Ill.: Charles Thomas, 1974).

10. Fort, *Pleasure-Seekers;* Goode, *Drugs in American Society.*

11. Dickson, "Bureaucracy and Morality."

12. Bonnie and Whitebread, *Marihuana Conviction.*

13. Ibid.; Patricia A. Morgan, "The Political Uses of Moral Reform" (Ph.D. diss., University of California at Santa Barbara, 1976).

14. Musto, *American Disease,* pp. 244-245.

15. Ibid.

16. Ibid., p. 223.

17. Helmer, *Drugs and Minority Oppression;* Helmer and Vietorisz, *Drug Use.*

18. Helmer, *Drugs and Minority Oppression,* pp. 55, 75.

19. In her exhaustive study of the history of California narcotics controls, Patricia Morgan has noted the lack of evidence to support Musto and Helmer. She concludes that "both of these accounts are in many ways misleading and incomplete" (Morgan, "Moral Reform," p. 74). Helmer, in fact, at first acknowledges that marihuana use had only a small place in the history of Anglo-Mexican relations, but he then seems to contradict himself when he pictures an antimarihuana ideology as the basis of anti-Mexican unity.

20. Bonnie and Whitebread, *Marihuana Conviction,* pp. 37, 56, 67, 69, 119, 124.

21. Cook, *Illegal Drug Use;* Gilbert Geis, "Social and Epidemiological Aspects of Marihuana Use," in *The New Social Drug,* ed. D. Smith, pp. 78-90; Bonnie and Whitebread, *Marihuana Conviction;* John F. Galliher, James L. McCartney, and Barbara E. Baum, "Nebraska's Marihuana Law: A Case of Unexpected Legislative Innovation," *Law and Society Review* 8 (1974):441-456; Michael P. Rosenthal, "The Legislative Response to Marihuana," *Journal of Drug Issues* 7 (1977):61-77; John F. Galliher and Linda Basilick, "Utah's Liberal Drug Laws: Structural Foundations and Triggering Events," *Social Problems* 26 (1979):284-297.

22. See John Kaplan, *Marijuana—The New Prohibition* (New York: World Publishing, 1970), p. 4; Cook, *Illegal Drug Use,* p. 225.

23. U.S. National Commission on Marihuana and Drug Abuse, *Marihuana: A Signal of Misunderstanding* (Washington, D.C.: U.S. Government Printing Office, 1972), p. 7.

24. Kaplan, *Marijuana,* pp. 4-5.

25. Cook, *Illegal Drug Use,* p. 225. Other proponents of the Hippie Hypothesis include Bonnie and Whitebread, *Marihuana Conviction,* p. 227; Richard Brotman and Frederic Suffet, "Marijuana Use," in *Drug Use in America: Problem in Perspective,* National Commission on Marihuana

and Drug Abuse (Washington, D.C.: U.S. Government Printing Office, 1973), Appendix I, pp. 1075-1110; Richard Brotman et al., "Drug Use Among Affluent High School Youth," in *Marijuana,* ed. Erich Goode (New York: Atherton Press, 1970), pp. 128-135; Erich Goode, "Marijuana and the Politics of Reality," in *The New Social Drug,* ed. D. Smith, pp. 168-186; Grinspoon, *Marihuana Reconsidered;* National Commission, *Marihuana,* pp. 1-9, 94-102.

MARIHUANA   3
BEFORE THE SIXTIES—
AN OVERVIEW

The marihuana issue prior to the mid-1960s was very different from the marihuana issue of today. Not only were the images of the drug and its users strikingly dissimilar but also the amount of attention given to the drug in those days was considerably less. Let us survey the pre-1960s period by examining these two issues, beginning with the attention given to the drug.

MAGNITUDE OF THE ISSUE

Marihuana use has been a major public issue in the United States since the mid-1960s. It has attracted front-page headlines, innumerable surveys of use and attitudes, a national commission report, and voluminous hearings. Few Americans would fail to recognize its name. This notoriety inevitably influences our efforts to understand the drug's prior history. We too easily assume that because marihuana use recently has been a major issue it always has been so. When we turn to the Marihuana Tax Act of 1937, for example, we may decide too readily that it must have riveted the attention of the media, the policymakers, and the populace.

Such, at least, has been the cursory conclusion of many who have studied marihuana in the 1930s. "By the late 1920s and early 1930s," Henry Brill reports, "there was widespread alarm about

this new drug problem."[1] Marihuana use is said to have generated
"mass hysteria," "front-page headlines," and "widespread journal-
istic interest and public anxiety."[2] The Federal Bureau of Narcotics's
efforts to produce national antimarihuana legislation is pictured as
an "all-out attack," and its antimarihuana campaign is said to
have reached "a high pitch" by the time of the congressional marihuana hearings in 1937.[3] Concern about marihuana use by Mexicans
in the Southwest in the 1930s is described as having been "intense,"
and a "marihuana ideology" is pictured as having been an important
part of anti-Mexican sentiment.[4] Others who have studied the period
make no explicit judgment on the magnitude of the issue, but their
references to the bureau's "publicity campaign" seem to imply that
marihuana did attract a great deal of attention.[5] The artificial group-
ing of newspaper articles, speeches, and hearings that inevitably
occurs in any serious study of marihuana also conveys this impression.

In fact, however, the opposite was true. Prior to the 1960s, marihuana was a nonissue in the United States nationally and in most
local areas. It hardly ever made headlines or became the subject of
highly publicized hearings and reports. Few persons knew or cared
about it, and marihuana laws were passed with minimal attention.
To document these claims, let us take a more systematic look at
the changing importance of the marihuana issue in the wider scope
of public discussion. Our findings will help us to evaluate the Anslinger
and the Mexican hypotheses.

We can begin by taking the relative frequency of articles on
marihuana in the *Readers' Guide to Periodical Literature* (to be
cited as RG) as an indicator of the overall amount of attention
given to the drug in public discussion. By comparing the frequency
of articles on marihuana in a particular time period with the frequency of articles on alcohol in the same period and the frequency
of articles on marihuana in other periods, we can ascertain how
important the marihuana issue was during that period.[6]

Table 1 presents the relevant data. The time periods given are
those covered by successive bound volumes of the *Readers' Guide.*
The first two columns list the annual frequency of articles on alcohol
and marihuana respectively in each period. The third column presents the ratio of marihuana articles to alcohol articles (the "mari-
huana/alcohol" ratio) in each period and the fourth column, the
ratio of the annual frequency of marihuana articles in the time

Table 1

ALCOHOL AND MARIHUANA ARTICLES IN *READERS' GUIDE,*
1890-1976

	Annual Frequency		Ratios	
Period[a]	Alcohol	Marihuana	Mar/Alc[b]	Mar/67-76 mean[c]
1890-1899	18	.3	.02	*[d]
1900-1904	30	0	*	*
1905-1909	45	0	*	*
1910-1914	42	.2	*	*
1915-1918	108	0	*	*
1919-1921	103	.3	*	*
1922-1924	95	0	*	*
1925-1928	142	.25	*	*
1929-1932	226	.28	*	*
1932-1935	159	0	*	*
1935-1937	51	2	.04	.06
1937-1939	46	8	.17	.25
1939-1941	46.5	2	.04	.06
1941-1943	53.5	.5	.01	.02
1943-1945	43	2	.05	.06
1945-1947	38	3.5	.09	.11
1947-1949	49.5	0	*	*
1949-1951	35	.5	.01	.02
1951-1953	32.5	2	.06	.06
1953-1955	44.5	.5	.01	.02
1955-1957	42	0	*	*
1957-1959	35.5	0	*	*
1959-1961	29.5	0	*	*
1961-1963	34	.5	.01	.02
1963-1965	39	.5	.01	.02

[a]Time periods are those covered by successive volumes of the *Readers' Guide*. From 1929 to 1943, the volumes begin in July of the first year; from 1945 to 1949, in May; from 1951 to 1953, in April; and from 1955 on, in March.

[b]Ratio of the frequency of articles on marihuana to the frequency of articles on alcohol for each period.

[c]Ratio of the annual frequency of articles on marihuana in each period prior to 1967 to the mean annual frequency of articles on marihuana during the 1967-1976 period, 31.4.

[d]Asterisk denotes a ratio of less than .01.

Table 1 (cont.)

ALCOHOL AND MARIHUANA ARTICLES IN *READERS' GUIDE,*
1890-1976

	Annual Frequency		Ratios	
Period[a]	Alcohol	Marihuana	Mar/Alc[b]	Mar/67-76 mean[c]
1965-1966	29	2	.07	.06
1966-1967	39	3	.08	.10
1967-1968	26	28	1.08	
1968-1969	33	30	.91	
1969-1970	21	44	2.10	
1970-1971	32	49	1.53	
1971-1972	20	52	2.60	
1972-1973	34	36	1.06	
1973-1974	37	22	.59	
1974-1975	36	13	.36	
1975-1976	47	23	.49	
1976-1977	40	17	.43	

periods prior to 1967 to the average number of articles appearing
yearly between 1967 and 1976, 31.4—the "marihuana/1967-1976
mean" ratio. The greater these ratios, the more important the
marihuana issue was at any particular time prior to the mid-1960s.

As the table shows, the annual frequency of articles on alcohol
in the RG increased dramatically from 30 in 1900-1904 to 108 in
1915-1918 and reached an apex of 226 in 1929-1932. With the repeal
of Prohibition, it dwindled from 159 in 1932-1935 to roughly one-
third that number, 51, in 1935-1937. In subsequent decades, the
annual frequency varied erratically from 53.5 in 1941-1943 to 21
in 1969-1970 to 47 in 1975-1976 but never again approached the
average for the Prohibition period—147 articles per year between
1919 and 1935.

Between 1890 and 1966, the RG indexed only fifty-five articles
on marihuana, with twenty-four, or nearly half, appearing between
1935 and 1941, around the time of the Marihuana Tax Act. Even
during that time, however, the annual frequency never went above
eight. In the 1950s, despite a general concern with drug use and a
rash of congressional hearings and special symposia, a mere six

articles appeared in the RG. Only with the increase in use by middle-class youth in the late 1960s and the associated rise of the antiwar movement and the Counterculture did marihuana receive much attention. The annual frequency of marihuana articles indexed in the RG jumped from three in 1966 to twenty-eight in 1967 and reached a peak of fifty-two in 1971 (almost equal to the total number of marihuana articles appearing in the RG prior to 1967).

Before the mid-1960s, the marihuana/alcohol ratio exceeded .10 only once, during 1937-1939. Even then, right after the Marihuana Tax Act, marihuana articles appeared only 17 percent as often as articles on alcohol. In thirteen of the twenty-seven time periods prior to 1967, the marihuana/alcohol ratio failed to reach .01. In 1967 this changed dramatically. The marihuana/alcohol ratio jumped to 1.08; and for the ensuing five years, marihuana articles appeared in the RG as often as or more often than articles on alcohol, the ratio reaching a peak of 2.60 in 1971. The ratio subsequently declined to .43, but still remained 2.5 times greater than the highest pre-1967 ratio.

The marihuana/1967-1976 mean ratio tells a similar story. It was less than .01 for fourteen of the twenty-seven time periods prior to 1967. It exceeded .05 in only eight periods and reached a maximum of a mere .25 in 1937-1939. Marihuana articles appeared prior to 1967 at only a small fraction of the rate of the 1967-1976 period.

In short, the RG data clearly imply that marihuana was an insignificant issue prior to the mid-1960s, at least when compared to either alcohol at the same time or marihuana after the mid-1960s. A closer look at the historical record confirms this conclusion.

Prior to the efforts of the Federal Bureau of Narcotics to publicize the evils of marihuana in the mid-1930s, the drug was virtually ignored on the national level. It was overlooked by two seminal pieces of federal drug legislation, the 1914 Harrison Act and the 1922 Narcotic Drugs Import-Export Act, and was not mentioned in the major drug studies of the late 1910s and the 1920s.[7] Although it was the subject of reports by the Department of Agriculture in 1917, a U.S. Canal Zone committee in 1925, and the surgeon general in 1929, none of these gained much attention or reflected widespread concern. Neither marihuana nor the Canal Zone report, for example, was mentioned anywhere in the annual reports of the Canal Zone's governor.[8]

On the local level, marihuana received just sporadic press attention. Only one episode in New Orleans in 1926 appears to have been of any significance. On October 17 of that year, the report of a major police attack on "vice and marihuana" made the front page of the *New Orleans Times-Picayune* as well as other local newspapers. Moreover, unlike newspapers elsewhere, the *Times-Picayune* did not feel compelled to define marihuana, thus clearly assuming its readers' knowledge of the substance.

Contrary to the Mexican Hypothesis, marihuana was not a major public issue in the Southwest in the 1920s or early 1930s. The numerous state antimarihuana laws in that region, for example, were usually passed in a perfunctory way with little attention or publicity. Floor debate was minimal and occasionally jocular; newspaper coverage was slight.[9]

Even in California, the drug appears to have been a nonissue during the 1920s and 1930s. Marihuana rarely was mentioned in anti-Mexican propaganda or in discussions of Mexicans and crime. It received little press coverage, and the few articles that appeared showed little familiarity with the drug. During the 1930s, for example, the *San Francisco Chronicle* printed about two articles per year on marihuana. Only one made the first page, and only two were feature articles in the magazine section. One of these, Bushnell Diamond's "Shocking New Menace to Nation's Youth" on January 24, 1937, described marihuana as a new drug, previously unknown to California: "Until last year, addiction seemed to be confined chiefly to New York, where it had been introduced by foreigners." The California Division of Narcotics Enforcement published its first marihuana pamphlet (*Marihuana—Our Newest Narcotic Menace*) only in 1939. It too stressed that marihuana use was unknown in California prior to the "last few years."[10]

Despite the bureau's publicity efforts, the notoriety of marihuana barely increased in the mid-1930s. The claims of advancing menace and the heated rhetoric that marked the bureau's publications, periodical articles, and the congressional hearings on the Marihuana Tax Act at the time belied the minuscule amount of attention actually given to the drug. In the year prior to the hearings held by the House of Representatives on the tax act in April 1937, five major newspapers—the *New York Times, Washington Post, Los Angeles Times, Denver Post,* and *Dallas Morning News*—published only one article apiece per month on marihuana, and only two of these sixty-one pieces made the front pages.[11]

The actual passage and signing of the antimarihuana legislation was greeted with nonchalance: The *New York Times*'s terse wire-service report on the signing outdid the *Los Angeles Times,* the *Chicago Tribune,* and the *New Orleans Times-Picayune,* all of which ignored both the passage and the signing. The *San Francisco Examiner* paid somewhat more attention, giving the House vote seven paragraphs on page two and the signing a five-line dispatch on the front page.[12] Neither the *American Year Book, Americana Annual,* nor *Britannica Book of the Year,* however, mentioned the Marihuana Tax Act in its summary of congressional activity for 1937. Compared to the growth of fascism abroad and conflicts over New Deal policies at home, marihuana simply was not newsworthy.[13]

In the decade or so following passage of the Marihuana Tax Act, the only major indication of concern over the drug came in 1939, when Mayor Fiorello LaGuardia appointed a special committee to investigate the marihuana problem in New York City. The LaGuardia Committee and its eventual report received little attention outside law enforcement and medical circles, however; and even in New York City, marihuana was not a major issue. The *New York Times* carried only a handful of articles per year on the drug, and most of these were perfunctory reports of arrests and seizures buried on the inside pages. It ignored the establishment of the LaGuardia Committee and relegated a summary of its 1945 report to the last page.[14]

The 1950s and early 1960s witnessed numerous congressional hearings, White House conferences, and special panels on drug use in general, but marihuana did not share the attention, as only two examples will prove. In April of 1951, the House Committee on Ways and Means held hearings on legislation to increase and consolidate the penalties for trafficking in illicit drugs—what became known as the Boggs Act. In 238 pages of testimony, there were only two discussions of marihuana, both of which occurred as brief digressions.[15] Eleven years later, at President Kennedy's White House Conference on Narcotic and Drug Abuse, marihuana again was conspicuous by its absence from the deliberations. Although it was mentioned at several points, there were only two sustained discussions of it: a two-page description of marihuana smuggling from Mexico and a short exchange over the dangers of marihuana. A comment during the conference by Alfred Lindesmith, a sociologist, accurately described the amount of attention given the drug:

Nothing has been said about marihuana, and my impression of marihuana has been that it is generally agreed that it presents a relatively trivial problem from a number of points of view.[16]

No one leapt to disagree.

Marihuana use thus was a very minor issue in the United States during the entire first six-and-a-half decades of the twentieth century. Between 1890 and 1966 periodical articles on marihuana appeared only a fraction as often as articles on alcohol during the same period or articles on marihuana in subsequent years. The drug was roundly ignored by newspapers and official hearings and reports. Even at the height of the marihuana "menace" in the late 1930s, the drug made hardly a ripple. The marihuana issue of the 1930s or 1950s was quantitatively far different from the marihuana issue of the late 1960s. The former was an obscure matter, the province of a few law enforcement officials and moralists; the latter was a major public issue.

This conclusion has implications for our discussion of both the Mexican and the Anslinger Hypotheses. Any effort to root the Marihuana Tax Act in political pressure arising from antimarihuana and anti-Mexican sentiment in the Southwest must take into account the fact that marihuana was not a major issue in that area in the 1920s and 1930s. There was no major surge of concern in the mid-1930s and little interest in the fate of the bureau's legislative efforts. The association of marihuana with Mexicans may have influenced discussion and policymaking on the national level in some way, but neither concern about marihuana in the Southwest nor pressure from that region on the bureau was very intense. Marihuana was not a prominent part of any anti-Mexican crusade nor central to any racial stereotype of Mexicans.

Any discussion of the successful entrepreneurship of the Bureau of Narcotics must also recognize the insignificance of the marihuana issue in the mid-1930s. The fact that marihuana was such a nonissue was a crucial factor in the success with which the relatively small, underfunded Narcotics Bureau shaped national marihuana policy. The less that people know or care about an issue, the more likely it is that a small organization can decisively shape the laws concerning that issue without trouble or resistance.

IMAGES OF DRUG AND USER

Although conceptions of marihuana and its users changed greatly between the late 1890s and the early 1960s, certain themes do mark the period as a whole. We can review these briefly by turning to our content analysis of the *Readers' Guide* articles for the period. Forty-seven articles were included in the sample for the 1890-1963 period. How they characterized marihuana and its users can be taken as representative of public discussion as a whole.

Marihuana was most commonly seen as dangerous and moderate use as impossible (see Table 2). Seventy-seven percent of the forty-four articles that addressed the issue regarded marihuana as dangerous, while 56 percent of the thirty-four articles that referred to moderate use deemed it impossible.

Table 2
DANGER AND MODERATE USE, 1890-1963
(Total N = 47)

Degree of Danger

Articles regarding marihuana as:

Dangerous	Not So Dangerous	Relevant N[a]
34 (77%)	10 (23%)	44 (100%)

Possibility of Moderate Use

Articles regarding moderate use as:

Impossible	Possible	Relevant N[a]
19 (56%)	15 (44%)	34 (100%)

[a]Relevant N refers to the total number of articles addressing the issue.

Marihuana was said to have a wide array of effects (see Table 3). Sixty-four percent of the forty-two articles that discussed specific effects mentioned a panoply of acute physical and psychological consequences—distortions of time and space perception, uncontrollable laughter, rapid movement of ideas, stimulation of the imagination, delusions of grandeur, hallucinations, loss of inhibitions, suggestibility, seizures, raving fits, irresistible impulses, and so forth. About 48 percent referred to the general effects of chronic use—"weakening of moral fiber," "disintegration of personality," "general instability, mental weakness, and finally insanity," and physical deterioration. Other effects such as addiction, passivity, stepping-stone, accidents, and debauchery were mentioned less often.

Table 3
EFFECTS, 1890-1963
(Total N = 47)

Effect	Articles Mentioning [a]
Violence	24 (57%)
Passivity	5 (12%)
Addiction	5 (12%)
Dependence	0
Stepping-stone	7 (17%)
Debauchery	4 (10%)
Accidents	2 (5%)
Unpredictability	5 (12%)
Miscellaneous acute effects	27 (64%)
Miscellaneous long-term effects	20 (48%)
Relevant N [b]	42 (100%)

[a] Percentages total more than 100 because many articles mention several effects.
[b] Relevant N refers to the total number of articles that discuss specific effects.

The one specific effect that received the most attention by itself, however, was violence, which was mentioned by 57 percent of the articles. It was virtually the only effect to receive protracted attention. It was often explicitly said to be the main or most important danger of marihuana use. Examples of marihuana-induced crimes were recited and ancient legends about marihuana and violence were recounted.

The marihuana user had two very different *social* identities (see Table 4). On the one hand, he was seen as a member of one of a number of marginal social groups; 46 percent of the twenty-six articles that spoke to this issue described him as Mexican or Spanish-

Table 4
USERS, 1890-1963

(Total N = 47)

Perceived Using Groups	Articles Mentioning[a]
Mexicans	12 (46%)
Blacks	6 (23%)
Bohemians	2 (8%)
Other marginal groups	8 (31%)
Total marginal groups	16 (62%)
Youth	16 (62%)
High-status youth	0
High-status adults	1 (4%)
Other respectable groups	8 (31%)
Total respectable groups	16 (62%)
Relevant N[b]	26 (100%)

[a]Percentages do not add up to 100 or equal the totals for marginal and respectable groups because many articles refer to several using groups.

[b]Relevant N refers to the total number of articles that identified at least one using group.

speaking (often a laborer), while others described him as black, Oriental, East Indian, or white déclassé. On the other hand, the marihuana user was seen by 62 percent of the articles as a youth, a school child, or a high-school student of indeterminate social class and race. The reason for this ambiguity is simply that particularly in the 1935-1940 period, marihuana was perceived to be spreading from the former groups to the latter groups.

This is but a survey. The details of the development of marihuana law and ideology prior to the mid-1960s is the subject of the next two chapters.

NOTES

1. Henry Brill, "Recurrent Patterns in the History of Drug Dependence and Some Interpretations," in *Drugs and Youth: Proceedings of the Rutgers Symposium on Drug Abuse,* ed. J. R. Wittenborn et al. (Springfield, Ill.: Charles Thomas, 1968), p. 22.

2. Lester Grinspoon, *Marihuana Reconsidered* (New York: Bantam,

1971), p. 23; David Solomon, ed., *The Marihuana Papers* (New York: New American Library, 1966), pp. xv-xvi; Richard M. Blum and associates, *Society and Drugs* (San Francisco: Jossey-Bass, 1969), p. 71.

3. David Smith, ed., *The New Social Drug* (Englewood Cliffs, N.J.: Prentice-Hall, 1970), p. 1; Roger Smith, "U.S. Marihuana Legislation and the Creation of a Social Problem," in *New Social Drug,* ed. D. Smith, p. 110.

4. David F. Musto, *The American Disease* (New Haven: Yale University Press, 1973), p. 219; John Helmer, *Drugs and Minority Oppression* (New York: Seabury Press, 1975), p. 75.

5. Alfred Lindesmith, *The Addict and the Law* (New York: Random House, 1965), p. 228; Edward M. Brecher et al., *Licit and Illicit Drugs* (Boston: Little, Brown, 1972), pp. 413-419.

6. See the Methodological Appendix for a more detailed discussion of the magnitude study.

7. Richard J. Bonnie and Charles Whitebread II, *The Marihuana Conviction* (Charlottesville: University of Virginia Press, 1974), pp. 49-56.

8. United States Canal Zone Governor, *Annual Report of the Governor of the Panama Canal Zone* (Washington, D.C.: U.S. Government Printing Office, 1923-1930).

9. Richard J. Bonnie and Charles Whitebread II, "History of Marihuana Legislation," in *Marihuana: A Signal of Misunderstanding,* ed. U.S. National Commission on Marihuana and Drug Abuse (Washington, D.C.: U.S. Government Printing Office, 1972), Appendix I, pp. 491-498.

10. Patricia A. Morgan, "The Political Uses of Moral Reform" (Ph.D. diss., University of California at Santa Barbara, 1978); California Division of Narcotics Enforcement, *Marihuana—Our Newest Narcotics Menace* (Sacramento: California State Printing Office, 1939).

11. Donald T. Dickson, "Bureaucracy and Morality," *Social Problems* 16 (1968):143-156; John F. Galliher and Allyn Walker, "The Puzzle of the Social Origins of the Marihuana Tax Act of 1937," *Social Problems* 24 (1977):367-376.

12. *New York Times,* 3 August 1937; *San Francisco Examiner,* 15 June 1937 and 3 August 1937.

13. In contrast, forty years later to the day, President Jimmy Carter's advocacy of marihuana decriminalization made front page headlines. See, for example, *San Francisco Chronicle,* 3 August 1977.

14. *New York Times,* 12 January 1945.

15. U.S., House of Representatives, Committee on Ways and Means, *Control of Narcotics, Marihuana, and Barbiturates,* 82d Cong., 1st sess., 1951.

16. White House Conference on Narcotic and Drug Abuse, *Proceedings* (Washington, D.C.: U.S. Government Printing Office, 1962), p. 165.

THE RISE OF THE KILLER WEED

4

The 1930s witnessed the consolidation of an image of marihuana as a "killer weed," the development of a consensus among those at all interested that the drug was a menace, and the passage of the Marihuana Tax Act. In this chapter we shall examine how all this came to pass.

INITIAL UNCERTAINTY

Prior to the 1930s, among those few who considered the issue, there was no consistent image of marihuana use and the problems it posed. The seven *Readers' Guide* articles before 1931 show few commonalities of perception and theme. Only three are concerned with nonmedical marihuana use in the United States. The other four include a clinical report by a physician of his own reactions to cannabis, an appropriately lurid account of "hachisch eating" in an unidentified European or Near Eastern setting, an editorial on the findings of the Indian Opium and Hemp commissions, and a discussion by the governor of the Sinai Province of Egypt on hashish smuggling in the area.[1]

There was, moreover, no one name for the drug itself. By the mid-1930s, it was known generally as "marihuana," but until then it had several identities. As a medical preparation and an object of scientific interest, it was "cannabis"; as an intoxicant found in Mexico and along the Texas border, it was "marihuana"; and as an Eastern drug identified with Arabs and Indians, it was "hashish" (or "hachisch" or "hash eesh") or "Indian hemp."

The multiplicity of terms implies that the drug had no settled social identity even in the accounts of domestic American use. To Alfred Lewis, a Hearst reporter and well-known writer on the Southwest, it was "marihuana" and very Mexican. To Carlton Simon, chief of New York City's narcotics division, it was "hash eesh," smuggled in by Turks and East Indians and rapidly becoming the latest "narcotics evil." In a 1926 *Literary Digest* account, the drug was both "hasheesh" and "marihuana."

Assessments of the drug's dangers also varied greatly. Some articles expressed no worry at all. The 1895 *Spectator* editorial applauded the Indian Hemp Commission's conclusion that the moderate use of hemp was harmless (and excessive use less dangerous than a similar indulgence in alcohol) and added its own dictum that the real problem lay not in the drug, but in the gluttony of the user. The 1926 *Literary Digest* article showed a similar lack of concern in reporting the Department of Agriculture's judgment that marihuana use "simply causes temporary elation, followed by depression and heavy sleep."

Other articles noted some negative or dangerous effects but did not generally condemn the drug. In his 1893 clinical report, Edward W. Scripture succinctly noted some "disagreeable effects," but managed, nevertheless, to regard cannabis simply as an object of scientific interest. E. B. Mawer described the widely unpredictable results of "hachisch eating" but concluded that "one may occasionally use it without any marked ill effect." Even Scudamore Jarvis, while describing his own efforts to quash hashish smuggling in the Sinai, regarded the drug as a "mild form of narcotic," which was dangerous only after "constant use."

Still other articles took a more negative view. Lewis recounted how marihuana made the user uncontrollably violent, and Simon described it as an unmitigated evil.

SOUTHWEST-NEW ORLEANS STEREOTYPE

The lack of consistency in subject matter, in the assessment of marihuana's dangers, and even in the names used to describe the drug suggests that for much of the first three decades of the century, there was no generally accepted conception of marihuana either as a drug or as a social problem. In the Southwest and New Orleans, however, such a unified image—tying together marihuana, violence, and Mexican laborers and other lower-class groups—had existed from the early 1910s.

Marihuana use, as we have shown in the previous chapter, was never a major issue in the Southwest at the time, nor was it an important part of anti-Mexican racial stereotypes. Mexican laborers, however, often were perceived by Anglos as "criminal types": They were noted for carrying knives and being drunk and disorderly. When marihuana was discussed, it was usually associated with Mexicans. As a result, marihuana also became associated with violence, a "killer weed."

The idea that marihuana use made Mexican laborers violent was well established among upper-strata Mexicans in both Mexico and the United States in the early 1900s.[2] As Mexicans moved into the United States to take the cheap laboring jobs available in fields from Texas to California and as far north as Idaho and Montana, they brought marihuana with them. The Mexican-marihuana-violence image then followed. Lewis's 1913 *Cosmopolitan* short story concerns the ill-fated adventures of an errant Harvard graduate who is attracted to Mexicans and marihuana in a border town and ultimately becomes so violent that he must be killed in self-defense. Lewis's narrator is quite clear that marihuana is a Mexican drug, and he is no less clear that marihuana induces violence and that Mexicans are worthless.

Once old marihuana wrops its tail about your intellects, you becomes voylent an' blood-hungry, an' goes on the onaccountable war-path, mighty deemoniac. . . .

Mexicans . . . ain't of no use in this world but to shoot at when you wants to unload an' clean your gun.[3]

The image of marihuana presented by Lewis was common whenever the drug was discussed in the Southwest in the 1910s and 1920s. Reports on marihuana by the U.S. Department of Agriculture in 1917 and by U.S. Canal Zone authorities in 1925 cite numerous accounts by law enforcement officials and newspapers in the Southwest regarding the connections between marihuana, Mexicans, and violence. The brief legislative discussions that preceded the passage of antimarihuana legislation in numerous southwestern and western states often made pointed references to the Mexican origins and violent effects of the drug. California crime studies in the 1920s noted the high rates of crime and delinquency among Mexicans, and the state's narcotics reports identified marihuana as a Mexican drug.[4]

The perception of marihuana as violence-producing also developed in places where Mexicans were not identified as the only users, principally in New Orleans. As we have noted, New Orleans was perhaps the one place in the 1920s and 1930s where marihuana was an issue of some importance. It is not surprising, then, that several local officials and citizens wrote pieces describing the evils of the drug: Frank Gomila, New Orleans commissioner of public safety; Eugene Stanley, New Orleans district attorney; and A. E. Fossier, a local physician. Their work had immense impact on the public discussion of marihuana in the 1930s and subsequent decades.[5]

The authors agreed that marihuana made the user violent. Indeed their perceptions are summed up neatly by the title of Stanley's article—"Marihuana as a Developer of Criminals." They did not, however, identify Mexicans as the sole users. Fossier and Stanley, whose articles were virtually identical, described the user simply as of the "criminal class." Gomila asserted that marihuana dealers were "Mexicans, Italians, Spanish-Americans, drifters from ships" and that users included dock workers and sailors, Negroes ("Practically every Negro in the city can give a recognizable description of the drug's effects"), Mexicans, and "vicious characters." The New Orleans image of marihuana and violence, in short, developed in tandem with a perception of the users as either members of racial minorities or as lower- and working-class whites.[6]

In the early 1930s, the New Orleans and Southwest image of marihuana use found its way into the discourse of federal law enforcement officials, and by 1935 it dominated media discussions of the drug as well. Prior to that time, marihuana had received little federal attention, and when it had, the Mexican-marihuana-violence connection was not evident. In 1929, both the federal act establishing "narcotics farms" for treating addicts and the surgeon general's report referred to the drug as "Indian hemp," not "marihuana." The surgeon general's discussion in particular seemed to draw its image of the drug solely from various Oriental legends and thus presented a dual image of its effects. From legends of amok Malays and Islamic assassins came an image of crime and violence; from stories of decadent, declining civilizations came an image of passivity and deterioration.[7]

In contrast, the 1931 "Report on Crime and the Foreign Born" by the National Commission on Law Observance and Enforcement (the Wickersham Commission) reflected but did not consistently endorse the New Orleans-Southwest stereotype of Mexicans-violence-marihuana. The report was concerned with whether or not the foreign born had higher crime rates than native-born white Americans. A review of official crime reports satisfied the researchers that nearly all foreign-born groups had lower crime rates than native-born whites. The exception was Mexicans, whose official crime rates were exceedingly high, and the report spent considerable time pondering this matter. Although it concluded that the high crime rates had more to do with social conditions, differential arrest rates, and cultural differences than with an inherent Mexican tendency to violence, the very attention given the Mexican-violence issue attests to the strength of the stereotype. Indeed, the researchers documented the prevalence of the prejudice with quotes from judges and police officials in areas with high Mexican populations.

The report also noted that Mexicans were tied closely to drug use, particularly marihuana use. Mexicans, it reported, constituted only 2.7 percent of all offenders in state and federal prisons, but 27.1 percent of all drug offenders. Marihuana was described as "a drug the use of which has spread with the dispersion of Mexican immigrants" and whose "use is widespread throughout Southern California among the Mexican population."[8]

Finally, marihuana was described as a violent drug in a citation from a publication of the California State Narcotics Committee: "If continued, the drug develops a delirious rage, causing the smoker to commit atrocious crimes."[9]

It was the New Orleans-Southwest stereotype that insinuated itself into the perceptions of federal narcotics officials. The Wickersham study and the 1917 Department of Agriculture investigation made their way into the bureau's files, and a New Orleans FBN agent forwarded Stanley's article to his superiors in Washington.[10] FBN Commissioner Harry Anslinger reported that his first perceptions of marihuana were based reports from southwestern and western states where there was concern about the behavior of Mexicans who "sheriffs and local police departments claimed got loaded on the stuff and caused a lot of trouble, stabbings, assaults, and so on."[11]

It is not surprising, then, that when federal narcotics officials first referred to marihuana, they described its users as "Spanish-speaking" and "Latin Americans."[12] Several years later, when the FBN began publicizing the effects of the drug, it stressed violent crime.[13]

In short, a stereotype connecting marihuana use, Mexican laborers and other lower-class groups, and violence developed in the Southwest and New Orleans in the 1910s and 1920s. This stereotype made its way into the federal bureaucracy through clear avenues of diffusion and from there into the national media. By the 1930s, whenever the drug was discussed, the intoxicating products of the hemp plant were clearly identified as "marihuana," which was perceived as a violence-inducing drug, first used in the United States by Mexican laborers and other marginal social groups. When the drug was seen to be spreading to "school children" in the mid-1930s, the Mexican component of the image became vestigial. Marihuana's reputation as a violence-producing weed, however, remained strong. Detached from its original social moorings, the image of marihuana as a "killer weed" became the mainstay of the bureau's case against the drug and through the bureau's efforts came to dominate virtually all discussion of marihuana for a considerable time.

THE BUREAU TAKES ON MARIHUANA

Once the bureau decided to act on marihuana, therefore, it had a ready-made image of the drug to disseminate. The bureau's decision, however, was the result of a complex set of events, and its relationship to marihuana was anything but simple or constant.

Prior to 1929, federal narcotics officials virtually ignored marihuana. Their semiannual and annual reports for 1926 through 1928 do not even mention it. In 1928, however, Congressman James O'Connor of New Orleans requested the inclusion of marihuana in the Harrison Act, and the next year, Senator Morris Sheppard of Texas proposed a bill to add the drug to the Narcotic Drugs Import and Export Act. These actions, coupled with the surgeon general's report and the new federal classification of marihuana as a narcotic, brought the drug to the attention of narcotics officials.[14]

Their initial official response, however, was cold indifference. The narcotics reports for 1929 and 1930 presented a perfunctory assessment of the drug and showed no recognition of its use bothering anyone. They noted the erstwhile domestic hemp industry, the widespread wild growth of the plant, the modest imports for legitimate medical use and occasionally for nonmedical use, and the availability of treatment for addicts at the federal narcotics farms. Finally, the reports briefly discussed marihuana "abuse":

The abuse of this drug consists principally in the smoking thereof, in the form of cigarettes for the narcotic effect. This abuse of the drug is noted particularly among the Latin-American or Spanish-speaking population. The sale of cannabis cigarettes occurs to a considerable degree in states along the Mexican border and in cities of the Southwest and West, as well as in New York City, and in fact wherever there are settlements of Latin Americans.[15]

There was no alarm and hardly a hint that there was a problem requiring the intervention of the fledging Federal Bureau of Narcotics.

In the reports for 1931 through 1934, the bureau's official tone became defensive; rather than simply ignoring any marihuana problem, it explicitly denied that there was one. In 1930, the bureau had been content simply to note the possibility of illicit imports; in 1931, it took pains to argue that these imports were minuscule and that federal controls were not yet needed. It also argued that the publicity given to the drug by unnamed "newspaper articles" was exaggerated.

A great deal of public interest has been aroused by newspaper articles appearing from time to time on the evils of the abuse of marihuana, or Indian hemp, and more attention has been focused upon specific cases reported of the abuse of the drug than would otherwise have been the case. This publicity tends to magnify the extent of the evil and lends color to an inference that there is an alarming spread of the improper use of the drug, whereas the actual increase in such use may not have been inordinately large.[16]

The bureau's official reluctance to regard marihuana use as a problem requiring immediate federal attention is interesting in light of the claims of the Anslinger and Mexican hypotheses. Had the bureau's eventual concern with marihuana derived simply from local political pressure (as the Mexican Hypothesis suggests) or from a moralistic desire to suppress a vice (as some versions of the Anslinger Hypothesis argue), it would have acted in the early 1930s. Its reports from those years clearly show that it sensed pressure for a national law, and Commissioner Anslinger personally regarded marihuana use as a vice requiring federal attention. From his first year as head of the FBN, his correspondence advocated eventual national controls.[17] The FBN, however, was neither a moral-crusading, expansion-seeking bureaucracy nor a simple pawn of external political pressure. It was primarily an organization attempting to survive in a basically inhospitable environment, and it did so by strictly limiting its purview. In a sense, it was thrice chastened—first by the failure of Prohibition, second by the court challenges to the Harrison Act, and third by the heavy weight of the Depression.

Commissioner Anslinger and many of the bureau's other top officials had been employees of the Prohibition Bureau, when it had had the responsibility for narcotics law enforcement in the 1920s. They thus had had a close look at the failure of alcohol control and had come away with a set of powerful lessons: Federal narcotics officials should not directly meddle in the lives of private citizens or seek to control any but the most clearly dangerous drugs. If they did, they risked fomenting public discontent and undermining their own legitimacy.[18]

The judicial history of the Harrison Act also predisposed the bureau to be circumspect in its activities. The Harrison Act was formally a revenue measure that sought to control narcotics by taxing transfers between registered parties and forbidding all transfers to those ineligible to register (virtually everyone but drug companies, physicians, and pharmacists). Between 1915 and 1930, the U.S. Supreme Court had been called on several times to interpret the act's intent.[19] In a few of these cases, the constitutionality of a tax law forbidding transfers of a taxed substance had become an issue, especially when the provision was used to prosecute physicians attempting to provide opiate addicts with maintenance doses of their drug. Although the act was never overturned, the bureau was reluctant to add a new drug to it or do anything else that could occasion yet another court challenge. The problems involved were discussed extensively by narcotics officials after the 1929 surgeon general's report on marihuana and were officially analyzed at the 1937 House hearings on the Marihuana Tax Act.[20]

Finally, the Bureau was hemmed in by the Depression. It faced the prospect of years of minimal budgets that could not support expanded activities. Indeed, its budget reached a peak of $1.7 million for the fiscal year ending June 30, 1933, and declined thereafter.[21]

Federal control of marihuana, moreover, presented its own special problems; in the early 1930s, no one could find a constitutional way to include it in either the Harrison Act or the Narcotic Drugs Import and Export Act. Since the former used the federal taxing power to control drug use, its constitutionality was based on the assumption that it generated significant revenue. By 1929, however, marihuana had virtually no medical uses and hence there was little licit trade to be taxed. The Narcotic Drugs Import and Export Act used the federal power over foreign commerce to control domestic drug use by employing the presumption that possession of a drug implied illegal importation. Marihuana, however, was grown largely domestically, so the presumption of importation would have been irrational and hence unconstitutional. Furthermore, any effort to control marihuana evoked opposition from pharmaceutical companies, the hemp industry, and the medical profession.[22]

For all these reasons, the bureau in the early 1930s attempted to limit its responsibility for day-to-day narcotics enforcement and to resist proposals for federal marihuana legislation. All things considered, it was often a resolutely reticent organization, not an aggressively expansionistic one. Its strategy was to have the states handle marihuana and deal with small-time narcotics offenders, while it made general policy and took care of large-scale trafficking.

The bureau sought to accomplish this governmental division of labor by getting the states to pass the Uniform Narcotic Drugs Act. The act had been under consideration for some seven years by a committee appointed by the National Conference of Commissioners on Uniform State Laws, when Commissioner Anslinger led the newly created FBN into the drafting process in 1931. He initially urged the inclusion of marihuana in the act but backed down in response to opposition from pharmaceutical companies, physicians, and the hemp industry. A final draft of the act, with a marihuana provision included only as a supplement, was approved in late 1932.

The bureau immediately began to lobby for state adoption of the act by sending its agents directly to legislators and by enlisting the help of sympathetic organizations—the Women's Christian Temperance Union, the World Narcotic Defense Association, the General Federation of Women's Clubs, and the Hearst press. Its efforts met with little success initially. By the end of 1934, only ten states had passed the act; opponents effectively pointed to its expense, its red tape, and its pretensions to control the medical profession and the pharmaceutical industry.

In response to this impasse, the bureau changed the thrust of its arguments and reversed its stand on the marihuana problem: Rather than insisting that the extent of marihuana use was exaggerated, it began to publicize the marihuana "menace" in its arguments for the Uniform Narcotic Drugs Act. The reversal is reflected in the bureau's reports for 1935 and 1936:

A problem which has proved most disquieting to the Bureau during the year is the rapid development of a widespread traffic in Indian hemp, or marihuana, throughout the country.[23]

The rapid development during the past several years, particularly during 1935 and 1936, of a widespread traffic in cannabis, or marihuana, as it is more commonly known in the United States, is regarded with much concern by the Bureau of Narcotics. Ten years ago there was little traffic in this drug except in parts of the Southwest. The weed now grows wild in almost every State in the Union, is easily obtainable, and has come into wide abuse.[24]

The emphasis on the marihuana menace appears to have been successful. Within a year, eighteen additional states had adopted the act, and those without previous legislation included the marihuana provision. At the same time, however, it undermined the bureau's effort to deflect pressure for federal controls. The modest increase in the attention given to marihuana as a result of the bureau's propaganda stimulated new demands for federal legislation and broke down bureaucratic resistance. In 1935, Senator Carl Hatch and Congressman John Dempsey of New Mexico introduced bills to prohibit the shipment and transportation of marihuana in interstate and foreign commerce. The bureau readied the usual objections, but this time it was overruled by the Treasury Department.

Consequently, by early 1936 the bureau had begun to search for an appropriate piece of legislation. Noting a recent Supreme Court decision upholding the National Firearms Act, which attempted to prohibit sales of machine guns by placing a $200 tax on each transfer, it settled on what would ultimately become the Marihuana Tax Act in early 1937: a proposal to place a prohibitive $100 per ounce tax on all sales of marihuana to nonmedical users, thus avoiding the constitutional objections to the Harrison Act.

Thus, the bureau became concerned with the marihuana problem and began to press for a federal law in a circuitous, paradoxical manner. Its general strategy was to survive in an unsupportive environment by strictly limiting its purview and not taking on any enforcement activities that might destroy its legitimacy or strain its resources. To these ends, it sought to make the states take responsibility for marihuana control as well as for day-to-day narcotics enforcement in general. Its efforts took the form of lobbying for state adoption of the Uniform Narcotic Drugs Act. To secure passage of this act, however, it had to conjure up the specter of a marihuana "menace." The added publicity given the drug made federal controls appear all the more necessary. In short, the bureau's efforts to avoid federal marihuana controls eventually led to its having to embrace them.

THE BUREAU'S CONSENSUS: MENACE, VIOLENCE, AND YOUTH

Once the bureau decided to act, it did so with little reserve, and its reticence gave way to a moral crusading fervor. Its antimarihuana publicity effort, though minuscule in the wider scheme of things, dominated public discussion of marihuana in the mid-1930s. Policymakers and the media faithfully adopted the bureau's image of marihuana, repeating the bureau's examples of marihuana-related violence and ignoring the data that the bureau chose to ignore.

The result was a striking consensus among those who discussed the drug. Marihuana was believed to be not just dangerous but a menace. Its myriad effects on consciousness were said to lead in various ways to a maniacal frenzy in which the user was likely to commit all kinds of unspeakable crimes. Users were identified both as Mexicans, who were the original users, and as youth to whom the drug was spreading. Concern focused on what the drug did to the latter group. High-school students were seen as the innocent victims of a drug that ultimately turned them into the worst kinds of criminals and ruined their lives. Indeed, the titles of articles from the period tell the whole story: "Marihuana Menaces Youth," "Marihuana: Assassin of Youth," "Youth Gone Loco," and "One More Peril for Youth."[25]

We can understand this consensus by looking at its various components—menace, violence, and youth—and by examining the nature of the bureau's hegemony.

The Menace

By the time they testified at the House hearings on the Marihuana Tax Act, federal narcotics officials were claiming that the whole nation was threatened by the marihuana "menace." Noting that "leading newspapers" had "recognized the seriousness of this problem," Clinton Hester, assistant general counsel for the Department of Treasury, opened the House hearings on the Marihuana Tax Act in April of 1937 by citing the following editorial from the *Washington Times:*

The marihuana cigaret is one of the most insidious of all forms of dope, largely because of the failure of the public to understand its fatal qualities. . . .

The nation is almost defenseless against it, having no Federal laws to cope with it and virtually no organized campaign for combatting it.[26]

Commissioner Anslinger underlined his portrayal of the drug as a "national menace" by contrasting it with opium, which could be both beneficial and harmful:

But here we have a drug that is not like opium. Opium has all of the good of Dr. Jekyll and all of the evil of Mr. Hyde. This drug is entirely the monster Hyde.[27]

The House Ways and Means Committee accepted Anslinger's portrait of marihuana and received with hostility the testimony of William Woodward, the AMA representative, who minimized the extent of the problem. Anslinger's view also dominated periodical articles during the period. All but one of the twenty-one articles that discussed the matter agreed that the drug was dangerous.

Marihuana was said to be a "serious menace" and "more dangerous than cocaine or heroin" by *Scientific American* and a "dangerous and devastating narcotic" by *Newsweek*.[28] The articles were almost equally as adamant that safe or moderate use of the drug was impossible; eleven of the fifteen articles that referred to the issue took this position. Indeed, only one article from the period, a 1936 *Literary Digest* piece, conveyed the sense that marihuana was fairly innocuous.[29] It described "sensuous pleasure" as the "beginning and end" of marihuana use and reported that Harlem reefer parties were generally affable and peaceful in contrast to the average alcohol party (see Table 5).

Table 5
DANGER AND MODERATE USE, 1935-1940
(Total N = 22)

Degree of Danger

Articles regarding marihuana as:

Dangerous	Not So Dangerous	Relevant N[a]
20 (95%)	1 (5%)	21 (100%)

Possibility of Moderate Use

Articles regarding moderate use as:

Impossible	Possible	Relevant N[a]
11 (73%)	4 (27%)	15 (100%)

[a]Relevant N refers to the total number of articles discussing the issue.

Violence

Although marihuana was said to produce a myriad of effects and was condemned as "unpredictable" in this regard, violence was the mainstay of arguments against the drug. In contrast to the claims of passivity that would dominate antimarihuana beliefs in the 1960s, marihuana was said to produce aggressive actions against self and others. Earl and Robert Rowell, in their 1939 antimarihuana tract, captured this image quite well: "While opium Kills ambition and Deadens initiative, marihuana incites to immorality and crime."[30] In the 1960s, marihuana would be said to "Kill ambition" and "Deaden initiative."

In one of its first detailed descriptions of the effects of marihuana, the FBN enumerated the drug's various effects on consciousness—euphoria, stimulation of the imagination, kaleidoscopic visions, distortions of time and space perception—and then argued:

The principal effect of the drug is upon the mind which seems to lose the power of directing and controlling thought. Its continued use produces pronounced mental deterioration in many cases. Its more immediate effect apparently is to remove the normal inhibitions of the individual and release any antisocial tendencies which may be present. Those who indulge in its habitual use eventually develop a delirious rage after its administration, during which time they are, temporarily at least, irresponsible and prone to commit violent crimes.[31]

While mental deterioration received no further attention, the violence theme was supported by quotes from appropriate authorities and by examples of "marihuana crimes."

At the House hearings, a large number of dangers again were noted, including unpredictability, degeneration of the brain, insanity, distortions of perception, automobile accidents, addiction, and death. Indeed, the only effect not imputed to marihuana was progression to harder drugs. The stepping-stone claim, which became the basis of the bureau's case against marihuana in the 1950s, was specifically denied by Anslinger.

Mr. Dingell. I am just wondering whether the marihuana addict graduates into a heroin, an opium, or a cocaine user.

Mr. Anslinger. No sir; I have not heard of a case of that kind. I think it is an entirely different class. The marihuana addict does not go in that direction.[32]

The hearings clearly stressed violence, however. Anslinger argued that marihuana use stimulated violent behavior by dissolving moral restraints, destroying the ability to judge right and wrong, stimulating grandiose fantasies, and making the user highly suggestible. He supported his case with a half-dozen examples of marihuana-related crimes, a study (from Stanley) that concluded that 125 of 450 inmates in a New Orleans jail were "marihuana addicts," and several Old World marihuana legends from Fossier and Stanley: that hashish was used by the Islamic sect of Assassins to fortify themselves for political murders, that it made the Malays run "amok," and that it was the "nepenthe" that Homer said "made men forget their homes." Violence was also the central theme of the three articles (including the Stanley and Gomila pieces) submitted as exhibits to the committee and two of the four letters submitted.[33] No other allegation received even a fraction of this attention.

Violence was the mainstay of periodical articles during the era also (see Table 6). Eighty-five percent of the twenty *Readers' Guide* articles that discussed effects mentioned violence. In contrast, only

Table 6
EFFECTS, 1935-1940
(Total N = 22)

Effect	*Articles Mentioning*[a]
Violence	17 (85%)
Passivity	3 (15%)
Addiction	4 (20%)
Dependence	0
Stepping-stone	2 (10%)
Debauchery	4 (20%)
Accidents	2 (10%)
Unpredictability	4 (20%)
Miscellaneous acute effects	17 (85%)
Miscellaneous long-term effects	15 (75%)
Relevant N[b]	20 (100%)

[a]Percentages total more than 100 because numerous articles mention several effects.
[b]Relevant N refers to the total number of articles mentioning at least one effect.

a few referred to addiction, passivity, stepping-stone, accidents, or other specific effects. More importantly, violence was virtually the only theme that received detailed attention. The claim was discussed at length and was buttressed by various legends and alleged cases of marihuana-induced crime.

We cannot adequately appreciate the importance of the violence claim in discussions of marihuana in the late 1930s, however, simply by noting how often the allegation was mentioned. Violence was not simply quantitatively predominant; it also provided the basis of the gestalt that organized perceptions of both the user and use.

Violence was seen not simply as the major effect of marihuana use but as the essential characteristic of the user as well. When periodicals described the user, they pictured either a violent fiend or an innocent victim turned violent fiend. None described him as either normal or essentially withdrawn and passive. Marihuana users were "criminals, degenerates, maniacs" in the words of *Survey Graphic* and *Forum and Century*.[34]

The violence claim also was a way of conceptually organizing and understanding the many other effects imputed to marihuana; each was primarily seen as a way in which marihuana made the user violent. As the 1936 FBN report put it, marihuana use generated violence by removing normal inhibitions and releasing antisocial tendencies. This twin theme of irresistible impulses and destruction of the will pervaded the literature.[35] In a 1937 article Anslinger restated this proposition in a way that linked violence to insanity:

Addicts may often develop a delirious rage during which they are temporarily and violently insane; . . . this insanity may take the form of a desire for self-destruction or a persecution complex to be satisfied only by the commission of some heinous crime.[36]

The persecution complex mentioned by Anslinger was said by others to arise from the delusions and hallucinations brought on by the drug. In his confusion, a user was likely to perceive imaginary threats from others and even fear that his best friend was out to kill him. He would naturally turn to violence to protect himself. Those not subject to delusions of persecution might be prone to "acute erotic visions," which would lead them to commit forcible rape.[37]

Even the most elementary effects of marihuana on consciousness took on a sinister cast. Simple distortions of time and space perception and disturbances of connected thought were said to confuse the mind in such a way that the "slightest impulse or suggestion carries it away." Heightened suggestibility itself was also regarded as a cause of violence, because it was used by "leaders of gangs and criminals" to lure the innocent into crime.[38]

In short, nearly every effect imputed to marihuana was also linked to violence and was interpreted in its light. Insanity, destruction of the will, suggestibility, distortions of perception, and alterations of consciousness all carried the connotations of violence and crime. The image of the violent criminal tied these disparate effects together and gave them coherence.

From Mexicans to Youth

The late 1930s had a dual image of the user. He was said to be on the one hand a Mexican or Spanish-speaking laborer, a black, or bohemian, or a member of the criminal classes—all low-status groups—and on the other hand, a youth of indeterminate social stratum. Eleven of the sixteen periodical articles that discussed the user's social identity mentioned one or more low-status groups, usually Mexicans, while thirteen mentioned youth or school children or high-school students (see Table 7).

The emphasis, however, was clearly on youth. The concern was

Table 7
USERS, 1935-1940

(Total N = 22)

Perceived Using Groups	Articles Mentioning[a]
Mexicans	9 (56%)
Blacks	4 (25%)
Bohemians	2 (13%)
Other marginal groups	5 (31%)
Total marginal groups	11 (69%)
Youth	13 (81%)
High-status youth	0
High-status adults	1 (6%)
Other respectable groups	5 (31%)
Total respectable groups	13 (81%)
Relevant N[b]	16 (100%)

[a]Percentages do not add up to 100, because some articles mention several using groups.

[b]Relevant N refers to the total number of articles mentioning at least one using group.

with what marihuana was doing to young people, not to Mexicans. "It is the useless destruction of youth which is so heartbreaking to all of us," said Anslinger.[39] While Mexicans were directly or indirectly identified as the source of the drug, they were then largely ignored. There were hardly any references to violent, degenerate Mexicans.

The FBN report for 1933 was the last to identify Spanish-speaking persons as marihuana users and the first to note youthful use: "A disconcerting development in quite a number of states is found in the apparently increasing use of marihuana by the younger element in the larger cities."[40] The concern with youthful use continued throughout the 1930s.

Concern for the youthful user also dominated the Marihuana Tax Act hearings.

[Marihuana] is now being used extensively by high-school children. . . . The fatal marihuana cigarette must be recognized as a deadly drug and American children must be protected against it. . . . The great majority of indulgers are ignorant and inexperienced youngsters. . . . We have had numerous reports of school children and young people using cigarettes made from this weed. . . . The National Congress of Parents and Teachers . . . is deeply concerned with increasing use of marihuana by children and youth.[41]

Mexicans, in contrast, were seldom mentioned at the hearings and then only in passing. At several points, marihuana was described as a drug introduced into the United States by Mexicans.[42] The violent behavior of Mexicans was described as the major issue only once and then in a letter from Floyd K. Baskette, city editor of the *Alamosa* (Colorado) *Daily Courier*. Baskette linked marihuana use to "hundreds" of violent crimes committed by Mexicans.[43] Though often quoted as characteristic of perceptions of marihuana at the time, the letter is important precisely because it was so unrepresentative. Indeed, what had turned marihuana use from a Southwest problem to a "national menace" was the perception not only of geographical expansion but also of spread of use to a new group—youth. The Marihuana Tax Act was passed not to punish Mexican users but to save youthful ones.

Although Mexicans were not the main object of concern, they still figured in the discussion of marihuana in other ways. They were identified as the original users of the drug and at times were implicated in its dissemination.

> The Mexican laborers have brought seeds of this plant into Montana and it is fast becoming a terrible menace. . . . We have numerous reports of school children and young people using cigarettes made from this weed.[44]

Properly speaking, moreover, marihuana was seen not as a "youthful drug" (as in the 1960s) but as a "drug infecting youth." It was seen not as indigenous to youthful culture and experience but as an alien intrusion. Youth were regarded not as the willful instigators of use but as innocent, ignorant victims seduced and destroyed by the drug and its wily peddlers.

> School children are the prey of peddlers who infest school neighborhoods. . . .High-school boys and girls buy the destructive weed without knowledge of its capacity for harm, and conscienceless dealers sell it with impunity. . . .The fatal marihuana cigarette must be recognized as a deadly drug and American children must be protected against it.[45]

> That youth has been selected by the peddlers of this poison as an especially fertile field makes it a problem of serious concern to every man and woman in America.[46]

In general, youthful marihuana users were seen as innocent victims who became violent fiends only after use.

In contrast, the images of infection and seduction of the innocent were rarely used in regard to Mexican laborers or other low-status users. Marihuana instead was seen as indigenous and appropriate to them. If anything, low-status users were seen as the carriers of infection and as the seducers.

Despite the emphasis on youthful marihuana users, therefore, perceptions of Mexican users still exerted a significant indirect influence on perceptions of the marihuana menace. Although concern focused on youthful use, the drug itself was seen as essentially belonging to low-status groups, and it accordingly was perceived as dangerous and criminogenic, alien and infecting.

FBN Hegemony

There was a wide consensus about marihuana in the late 1930s among those few who discussed the drug: It was dangerous; it caused violent crime; it threatened the nation's youth. This consensus did not reflect a simple convergence of several independent assessments of the available evidence. Instead, it was largely created by the FBN, which effectively dominated public discussion of marihuana. The periodical articles of the period drew explicitly or implicitly on the bureau's own information and the sources that it favored, while ignoring what the bureau ignored. This happened precisely because there was no "national menace" and hence few persons knew about the drug. In such circumstances, the bureau was one of the only sources of information.

The clearest manifestation of the bureau's hegemony is that all of the articles sound the same. They make the same claims in virtually the same language. Marihuana, we are told again and again, was a problem only in the Southwest until "three or four" years ago, when it became a "national menace." It is the same as hashish, the Oriental drug of assassins. It is "more dangerous than cocaine or heroin." It is spread by evil peddlers to thrill-seeking youth and so on. One cannot read through the literature of the period without a recurring feeling of *deja vu.*

When we examine this uniformity closely, we can identify specific lines of influence. We have already seen that the New Orleans articles by Stanley, Fossier, and Gomila figured heavily in the FBN's arguments against marihuana. The Gomila and Stanley articles found their way into the Marihuana Tax Act hearings, and Anslinger incorporated a prisoner study and the various Old World myths recounted by Stanley into his own writing and testimony.[47]

The periodical articles of the period were also influenced heavily by the New Orleans information, either directly or indirectly through the bureau. Several repeated almost verbatim the Old World marihuana legends, while others cited the Stanley prisoner study. A two-fold crime theory presented by Gomila—that marihuana both caused unpremeditated violence and was used by criminals to fortify themselves for premeditated crimes—also was mentioned.[48]

New Orleans, moreover, was the home of Robert P. Walton, a professor at the Tulane University School of Medicine, whose *Marihuana: America's New Drug Problem* was the decade's most comprehensive work on marihuana. Walton acknowledged learning about marihuana in New Orleans and reprinted the Gomila article as a definitive statement of the current state of the marihuana problem in the United States. His analysis followed the New Orleans-FBN assumptions by stressing menace, crime, and youthful use. Walton, in turn, directly influenced at least two articles, which reviewed his work and endorsed his conclusions.[49]

The direct influence of the FBN is just as clear. Besides the one article actually coauthored by Anslinger, seven articles explicitly credited the bureau or its commissioner as a source of information. The bureau's examples of marihuana crimes, moreover, were repeated incessantly—the Texas hitchhiker who murdered a motorist, the West Virginia man who raped a nine-year-old girl, the Florida youth who murdered his family with an ax, the Ohio juvenile gang that committed thirty-eight armed robberies, the Michigan man who killed a state trooper, and other equally bloodcurdling tales. The frequent repetition of the same criminal cases, most of which first appeared in Anslinger's 1937 article, is one of the clearest pieces of evidence that the articles drew upon a common source. Finally, the bureau's idiosyncratic insistence on informing the public that Mexican marihuana was indeed the same as Oriental hashish was mirrored in several additional articles.[50]

In sum, sixteen of the twenty-two articles in the *Readers' Guide* sample from 1935 to 1940 bear the mark of the FBN or its favored sources in one or more of the ways described above. The six that do not, moreover, serve to underline the bureau's importance in shaping marihuana beliefs. One of the articles was not about marihuana use in the United States at all but instead reported on hashish smuggling in Egypt. Another three discussed marihuana use in America but deviated from the established consensus in some way: Two drew on the work of Walter Bromberg of New York's Bellevue Hospital and described marihuana as fairly innocuous; a third characterized marihuana as dangerous but found claims of youthful use "unfounded."[51] In short, the exceptions merely prove the rule. The pervasive belief that marihuana use in America was dangerous, violent, and a threat to youth was decisively shaped by the Federal Bureau of Narcotics. The articles not influenced by the bureau either do not discuss American use or stand outside the dominant consensus about that use.

The FBN's hegemony also can be demonstrated by noting the

evidence that generally was not cited. Just as periodical articles generally used the information propagated by the bureau, they virtually ignored the information that the bureau ignored. Studies by the Indian Hemp Commission in 1894, the U.S. Canal Zone Committee in 1926 and 1933, and Walter Bromberg in 1934, all of which distinctly downplayed the dangers of marihuana use, were rarely mentioned during the period. Walton alluded to the first two in his marihuana volume but did not take them seriously. Only two articles made use of Bromberg's findings. This may seem odd, since the three studies not only were available and obviously known but also constituted the most systematic work done on marihuana use to that time. The bureau, however, found their findings uncongenial to its own position and was able to drown them with silence. It never mentioned either the Indian or the Canal Zone study, and Anslinger made only one questionable reference to Bromberg in response to the questions of the House Committee on Ways and Means. Asked if Bromberg validated the marihuana-crime link, Anslinger argued that Bromberg hedged his conclusions and that his study, based as it was on a prison population, was unreliable. Both arguments were misleading. Anslinger himself accepted a secondhand report of the New Orleans study, which also was based on a limited sample of prisoners. Bromberg did not hedge his conclusions: He explicitly argued that the contribution of marihuana use to crime was greatly exaggerated.[52]

The most important consequence of the bureau's domination over marihuana beliefs was that no one really opposed its efforts to procure a federal antimarihuana law. At the House hearings on the Marihuana Tax Act, for example, the opposition that surfaced was largely technical. Manufacturers of rope, hempseed, and hemp oil were concerned that their industries would be hampered by the law and were mollified by some minor changes in the text.[53] William Woodward, the American Medical Association representative, seemed to object to the act on the wider grounds that marihuana use was not really a problem and that a federal law would unduly restrict future research on marihuana. These issues, however, were *not* the central concern of the AMA. Woodward used most of his testimony to object to the additional tax and registration burdens that a separate marihuana law would place on physicians. In his letter to the Senate hearings, moreover, these burdens were the only objections that he raised to the act. The narrow, technical nature of the AMA's objection to the act becomes even clearer when we realize that Woodward advocated including marihuana in the already existing Harrison Act. Such a move would have restricted research as much as a separate marihuana act and would have been just as irrational if marihuana use were not a real problem. Clearly, neither of these points was basic to the AMA's objection. Physicians did not oppose a federal law against marihuana; they merely wanted it in a form that would place the least financial and administrative burden on them.[54] The bureau's dominance of the marihuana issue was complete.

NOTES

1. Edward W. Scripture, "Consciousness Under the Influence of Cannabis," *Science,* 27 October 1893, pp. 233-234; E. B. Mawer, "Hachisch Eating," *Cornhill Magazine,* May 1894, pp. 500-505; "Reports on Opium and Hemp," *Spectator,* 27 April 1895, pp. 570-571; Alfred H. Lewis, "Marihuana," *Cosmopolitan,* October 1913, pp. 645-655; Carlton Simon, "From Opium to Hash Eesh: Startling Facts Regarding the Narcotics Evil and Its Many Ramifications Throughout the World," *Scientific American,* November 1921, pp. 14-15; "Our Home Hasheesh Crop," *Literary Digest,* 3 April 1926, pp. 64-65; Scudamore Jarvis, "Hashish Smugglers of Egypt," *Asia,* June 1930, pp. 440-444. Both *Spectator* and *Cornhill Magazine* are British publications, but their presence in the *Readers' Guide* suggests that they were available to the reading public in the United States.

2. Richard J. Bonnie and Charles Whitebread II, *The Marihuana Conviction* (Charlottesville: University of Virginia Press, 1974), pp. 35-36; David F. Musto, *The American Disease* (New Haven: Yale University Press, 1973), p. 330.

3. Lewis, "Marihuana," p. 648.

4. Bonnie and Whitebread, *Marihuana Conviction,* pp. 32-38; Patricia A. Morgan, "The Political Uses of Moral Reform" (Ph.D. diss., University of California at Santa Barbara, 1978), pp. 82-83. The Agriculture Department, charged with enforcing the domestic provisions of the Food and Drug Act, commissioned its 1917 investigation to determine what effect the Treasury Department's 1915 ban on importation of cannabis for non-medical use (under the import-export provisions of the same act) had had on domestic use. The Canal Zone report was made by a special committee established to study marihuana use in the Canal Zone. The committee took a wider view of the issue and gathered information on use elsewhere as well.

5. A. E. Fossier, "The Marihuana Menace," *New Orleans Medical and Surgical Journal* 84 (1931):247-252; Frank Gomila and Madeline Lambou, "Present Status of the Marihuana Vice in the United States," c. 1931, reprint in *Marihuana,* ed. Robert P. Walton (Philadelphia: J. B. Lippincott, 1938), pp. 27-39; Eugene Stanley, "Marihuana as a Developer of Criminals," *Journal of Police Science* 2 (1931):256. The Gomila article originally appeared sometime in the early 1930s and was reprinted later by Walton.

6. The New Orleans articles also warned that marihuana use was spreading from these groups to school children, thus conveying an image of infection that would become important in marihuana consensus of the 1930s.

7. Oriental legends are recounted also by Stanley and Fossier and figure heavily in the bureau's case against marihuana in the 1930s and later. These legends by themselves, however, cannot account for the dominant image of marihuana as a violence-producing drug, since they provide "evidence" for a number of stereotypes about the drug. The predominance of the violence stereotype was the unique contribution of New Orleans and the Southwest.

8. U.S., National Commission on Law Observance and Enforcement, *Crime and the Foreign Born* (Washington, D.C.: U.S. Government Printing Office, 1931), pp. 154, 205.

9. Ibid., p. 205.

10. Bonnie and Whitebread, *Marihuana Conviction,* pp. 70-77, 312.

11. Cited in Musto, *American Disease,* p. 222.

12. U.S., Federal Bureau of Narcotics, *Traffic in Opium and Other Dangerous Drugs,* 1929 (Washington, D.C.: U.S. Government Printing Office), p. 15. The annual reports of the bureau are identified by the year they cover, not the year they were published.

13. Ibid., 1936, pp. 59-60.

14. Bonnie and Whitebread, *Marihuana Conviction,* pp. 56-59.

15. Bureau of Narcotics, *Traffic,* 1929, p. 15.

16. Ibid., 1931, p. 51.

17. Bonnie and Whitebread, *Marihuana Conviction,* p. 63.

18. Musto, *American Disease,* p. 213.

19. Alfred Lindesmith, *The Addict and the Law* (New York: Random House, 1965); Musto, *American Disease.*

20. Bonnie and Whitebread, *Marihuana Conviction,* pp. 60-61; U.S., House of Representatives, Committee on Ways and Means, *Taxation of Marihuana,* 75th Cong., 1st sess., 1937, pp. 7-8.

21. Donald T. Dickson, "Bureaucracy and Morality," *Social Problems* 16 (1968):143-156.

22. This and the following paragraphs draw upon Bonnie and Whitebread, *Marihuana Conviction,* pp. 56-126; and Morgan, "Moral Reform."

23. Bureau of Narcotics, *Traffic,* 1935, p. v.

24. Ibid., 1936, p. 57.

25. "Marihuana Menaces Youth," *Scientific American,* March 1936, pp. 150-151; Harry J. Anslinger and Courtney R. Cooper, "Marihuana: Assassin of Youth," *American Magazine,* July 1937, pp. 18-19, 150-153; Wayne Gard, "Youth Gone Loco," *The Christian Century,* 29 June 1938, pp. 812-813; Henry G. Leach, "One More Peril for Youth," *Forum and Century,* January 1939, pp. 1-2.

26. House of Representatives, *Taxation of Marihuana,* p. 6.

27. Ibid., p. 19.

28. "Marihuana Menaces Youth," *Scientific American;* "Marihuana More Dangerous Than Heroin or Cocaine," *Scientific American,* May 1938, p. 293; "New Federal Tax Hits Dealings in Potent Weed," *Newsweek,* 14 August 1937, pp. 22-23.

29. "Facts and Fancies About Marihuana," *Literary Digest,* 24 October 1936, pp. 7-8.

30. Earl A. Rowell and Robert Rowell, *On the Trail of Marihuana: The Weed of Madness* (Mountain View, Calif.: Pacific Press, 1939), p. 83.

31. Bureau of Narcotics, *Traffic,* 1936, pp. 59-60.

32. House of Representatives, *Taxation of Marihuana,* p. 24. At the shorter Senate hearings, Anslinger added that the marihuana user was much younger than the opium user. U.S., Senate, Finance Committee, *Taxation of Marihuana,* 75th Cong., 1st sess., 1937, pp. 14-15.

33. House of Representatives, *Taxation of Marihuana,* pp. 18-45, 123-124.

34. "Danger," *Survey Graphic,* April 1938, p. 221; Leach, "Peril for Youth."

35. George R. McCormack, "Marihuana," *Hygeia,* October 1937, pp. 898-899; "Marihuana More Dangerous Than Cocaine or Heroin," *Scientific American,* p. 293; "Marihuana," *Journal of Home Economics,* September 1938, pp. 477-479; "Marihuana Smoking Seen as Epidemic Among the Idle," *Science News Letter,* 26 November 1938, p. 340; Maud A. Marshall, "Marihuana," *American Scholar,* January 1939, pp. 95-101; Roger Adams, "Marihuana," *Science,* 9 August 1940, pp. 115-119.

36. Anslinger and Cooper, "Assassin of Youth," p. 150.

37. McCormack, "Marihuana," p. 899; Rowell and Rowell, *Trail of Marihuana,* p. 39.

38. "Marihuana More Dangerous Than Heroin or Cocaine," *Scientific American,* p. 293; Rowell and Rowell, *Trail of Marihuana,* p. 41.

39. Anslinger and Cooper, "Assassin of Youth," p. 150.

40. Bureau of Narcotics, *Traffic,* 1933, p. 36; 1937, p. 54; 1938, pp. 51-52.

The Strange Career of Marihuana

House of Representatives, *Taxation of Marihuana,* pp. 6, 35, 45.
42. Ibid., pp. 18, 45, 123.
43. Ibid., p. 32. The Baskette letter and a 1935 letter to the *New York Times* from C. M. Goethe of Sacramento are the two pieces of evidence cited by Musto (*American Disease,* pp. 220, 223) to support his contention that anti-Mexican sentiment was behind the Marihuana Tax Act.
44. House of Representatives, *Taxation of Marihuana,* p. 45. See also Albert Parry, "The Menace of Marihuana," *The American Mercury,* December 1935, pp. 487-490; William Wolf, "Uncle Sam Fights a New Drug Menace . . . Marijuana," *Popular Science Monthly,* May 1936, pp. 14-15; Anslinger and Cooper, "Assassin of Youth"; McCormack, "Marihuana"; Gard, "Youth Gone Loco"; "Marihuana," *Journal of Home Economics.*
45. House of Representatives, *Taxation of Marihuana,* p. 6.
46. Anslinger and Cooper, "Assassin of Youth," p. 18. For other references to youth as innocent victims, see McCormack, "Marihuana"; "Danger," *Survey Graphic;* Clair A. Brown, "Marihuana," *Nature,* May 1938, pp. 271-272; Marshall, "Marihuana"; Adams, "Marihuana."
47. House of Representatives, *Taxation of Marihuana,* pp. 18-31; Anslinger and Cooper, "Assassin of Youth."
48. Parry, "Menace of Marihuana"; "Marihuana Menaces Youth," *Scientific American;* Wolf, "Uncle Sam Fights a New Drug Menace"; Anslinger and Cooper, "Assassin of Youth"; Clarence W. Beck, "Marijuana Menace," *Literary Digest,* 1 January 1938, p. 26; Gard, "Youth Gone Loco"; Marshall, "Marihuana."
49. Walton, *Marihuana;* "Marihuana Smoking Seen as Epidemic," *Science News Letter;* "The History of Marihuana," *Newsweek,* 28 November 1938, p. 29.
50. Articles directly crediting the bureau or Anslinger: McCormack, "Marihuana"; "Marihuana More Dangerous Than Heroin or Cocaine," *Scientific American;* Brown, "Marihuana"; Gard, "Youth Gone Loco"; "Marihuana," *Journal of Home Economics;* Leach, "One More Peril for Youth"; S. R. Winters, "Marihuana," *Hygeia,* October 1940, pp. 885-887. Among the articles repeating examples of crimes are Parry, "Menace of Marihuana"; Beck, "Marihuana Menace"; "Danger," *Survey Graphic;* "Marihuana Smoking Seen as Epidemic Among the Idle," *Science News Letter;* Marshall, "Marihuana."
51. C. S. Jarvis, "Hashish Smuggling in Egypt," *The Living Age,* January 1938, pp. 442-447; "Facts and Fancies About Marihuana," *Literary Digest;* "Marihuana Gives Some a Jag," *Science News Letter,* 14 January 1939, p. 30; "Potent Weed," *Newsweek.*
52. House of Representatives, *Taxation of Marihuana,* p. 24; Walter

Bromberg, "Marihuana Intoxication," *American Journal of Psychiatry* 91 (1934):303-330 (see especially pp. 307-309).
    53. House of Representatives, *Taxation of Marihuana,* pp. 59-64, 67-86.
    54. Ibid., pp. 87-121; Senate, *Taxation of Marihuana,* pp. 33-34. Bonnie and Whitebread (*Marihuana Conviction,* pp. 164-169) and almost everyone else have erroneously painted Woodward as a patron of science and a major opponent of the bureau's hysterical view of marihuana. A closer reading of his House testimony and his Senate letter clearly shows that he was no such thing.

THE CONSENSUS REFINED

5

As the 1930s waned, marihuana was a "killer weed"; the Marihuana Tax Act was federal law; and a bureau-engineered consensus dominated public discussion. In the ensuing two decades or so, the "killer weed" image was supplemented, but not wholly displaced, by the claim that marihuana led to harder drugs. Laws against marihuana use got tougher, and the bureau's consensus persisted with important changes.

MODEST RETRENCHMENT AND THE LAGUARDIA DEBATE

Although the public discussion of marihuana in the 1940s was different from that of the 1930s in important ways, it is ultimately the similarities that are more striking. To be sure, marihuana generally was no longer seen as a rampant menace; it was rarely said to be an epidemic among school children; and its addicting, violence-generating, and mind-destroying qualities were sometimes questioned. Nevertheless, marihuana continued to be seen as a dangerous drug. No matter how strenuously the specific deleterious effects of the drug were denied, hardly anyone suggested that the Marihuana Tax Act should be repealed. The FBN's domination of marihuana beliefs and policy, if challenged in theory, remained solid in practice.

The withdrawal of the menace imagery was begun by the bureau itself in the late 1930s. Having procured the Marihuana Tax Act and thus gained ownership of the marihuana problem, the FBN no longer had an interest in portraying marihuana use as an epidemic out of control. Such a characterization, useful in obtaining federal legislation a few years before, now would have suggested that the bureau was failing in its law enforcement efforts. In any case, the FBN quickly dropped the tone of panic from its reports, which from 1937 through 1940 portrayed marihuana use as a serious problem that nonetheless was being brought under control. In its report for 1938, for example, the bureau spoke glowingly of the progress of law enforcement officials on various levels in eradicating marihuana traffic and educating the public about "the extremely pernicious effects of marihuana smoking." It concluded that these efforts had "unquestionably . . . discouraged any attempt to organize the illicit traffic on a large scale."[1]

The bureau also actively discouraged the kind of sensational publicity that it had purveyed just a few years before. It endorsed the following recommendation of the Women's Christian Temperance Union:

That publicity on marihuana be tempered to conform to the factual problem. That the importance of obtaining the cooperation of the public with the authorities in the suppression of the marihuana traffic and in destroying marihuana themselves under the guidance of officials, be stressed in educational campaigns rather than the dissemination of information regarding the effects of the drug which is apt to arouse curiosity or to cause sensational publicity.[2]

The effort to de-sensationalize marihuana in the 1940s no doubt went much further than the bureau wanted. Of eight periodical articles in the sample from 1941 to 1948 that focused on the deleterious effects of marihuana, six downplayed the dangers of the drug. Robert P. Walton, writing in *Science,* belatedly pointed out that the findings of each major scientific study of marihuana (those by the Indian Hemp Commission, the Canal Zone Committee, and the LaGuardia Committee) "have tended to minimize the gravity of the marihuana problem." *Science Digest* cited research concluding that "the behavior of the marihuana smoker is of a friendly, sociable character." Finally, *Time* opined that "despite its lurid

reputation, marihuana seems no more harmful than alcohol."
None of the articles, however, challenged the illegality of marihuana
or criticized the bureau's enforcement activity.[3]

What periodical articles said about marihuana during the 1940s
was largely a reflection of the debate over the LaGuardia Report,
which took place in the pages of the *American Journal of Psychiatry*
and the *Journal of the American Medical Association* (JAMA).
Indeed, four of the eight articles referred to the LaGuardia findings.[4]
To understand what was said about marihuana in the 1940s and the
bureau's role therein, we shall review this debate.

Fiorello LaGuardia, mayor of New York City, responded to the
1930s accounts of marihuana menace with some skepticism. From
his tenure in Congress, he recalled the conclusions of the Canal
Zone Report, which had "emphasized the relative harmlessness
of the drug and the fact that it played a very little role, if any, in
problems of delinquency and crime in the Canal Zone."[5] LaGuardia,
therefore, turned to the New York Academy of Medicine for expert opinion on the drug. The academy reported that a review of
the existing literature and conferences with city officials provided
no consistent conclusions about the dangers of marihuana or the
extent of its use in New York City.

In January 1939 LaGuardia responded by appointing the Mayor's
Committee on Marihuana, which consisted of members of the
academy and city officials. In the next six years, the committee
carried out extensive research on marihuana. A pharmacological
study attempted to isolate the psychoactive components of cannabis;
a clinical study observed the psychological and physiological effects
of a cannabis extract on seventy-seven volunteers (mostly prisoners)
in an experimental setting; and a sociological study used participant-
observation research by specially trained police personnel to look at
marihuana use in natural settings. A preliminary report, discussing
the clinical study, appeared in the *American Journal of Psychiatry*
under the authorship of Samuel Allentuck and Karl Bowman in
1942. The final report was released in January 1945.

The LaGuardia Report challenged most of the claims made against
marihuana. Although Allentuck and Bowman noted that marihuana
might release antisocial tendencies and could precipitate a psychosis
in the mentally unstable, they concluded that marihuana use did
not tend to excess, was not addicting, did not seriously disturb

mental or physical functioning, and did not lead to violence or to harder drugs. They also suggested that marihuana might be useful in facilitating opiate withdrawal and in treating depression and loss of appetite. They summed up their position as follows:

Prolonged use of the drug does not lead to physical, mental or moral degeneration, nor have we observed any permanent deleterious effects from its continued use. Quite the contrary, marihuana and its derivatives and allied synthetics have potentially valuable therapeutic applications which merit future investigation.[6]

The response to Allentuck and Bowman in the scientific community was initially positive. In a discussion accompanying their articles, Lawrence Kolb of the Public Health Service praised both the LaGuardia Committee and "Dr. Allentuck's timely paper" for helping the physician wade through the "misinformation and alarm that has gotten abroad about marihuana." He noted with appreciation the Allentuck-Bowman conclusions on the dangers of the drug, though he cited some reservations. For example, on the matter of crime, Kolb agreed that marihuana as then used in the United States did not contribute to crime, but he added that under some circumstances it might:

It can readily be seen that a drug which produces all these effects, if used as widely as alcohol is used in this country, might be like alcohol a very important contributing cause to crimes of various kinds.[7]

He concluded by warning against the use of marihuana to treat neurosis or drug addiction.

In a December 1942 editorial, JAMA struck an even more positive note. It accepted the Allentuck-Bowman refutation of prevailing beliefs about the dangers of marihuana and viewed with some enthusiasm the suggested therapeutic applications:

The preliminary clinical experiments by Dr. Allentuck with a group of drug addicts yielded encouraging results. A more exhaustive study of the possibilities of these drugs as a means of relieving withdrawal symptoms in narcotic addicts would seem to be justified.[8]

Like Kolb, the 1942 JAMA editorial welcomed the Allentuck-Bowman study as part of an ongoing scientific effort to create a reliable, coherent picture of marihuana use. It did not discuss the political impact of the study at all.

The response of law enforcement officials was quite different. In a January 1943 letter to the editor, Commissioner Anslinger largely condemned the report. While noting that the study confirmed the prevalent beliefs that marihuana precipitated psychosis and lowered inhibitions, thus leading to crime, he clearly voiced his general dissatisfaction.

From that point of view [of law enforcement] we feel that it is very unfortunate that Drs. Allentuck and Bowman should have stated so unqualifiedly that use of marihuana does not lead to physical, mental or moral degeneration and that no permanent deleterious effects from its continued use were observed. . . . More undiscriminating readers are perhaps likely to interpret the statement as the final word of the medical profession. Also there may well be some unsavory persons engaged in the illicit marihuana trade who will make use of the statement in pushing their dangerous traffic.[9]

Anslinger, then, was worried that any nonnegative assertion about marihuana would encourage use and hamper law enforcement. His concern about the consequences of the study led him to question its validity. He noted that the study's conclusions were based on research on a mere seventy-seven subjects, all of them prisoners, and provided a long list of quotations from other sources contradicting the study's findings. Finally, he cited Kolb's warning about therapeutic applications and quoted him as saying "that use of marihuana may be an important contributory cause to crime" without explaining the context of these remarks.[10]

Over a year later, Jules Bouquet, a member of the Narcotics Commission of the League of Nations and an oft-quoted colleague of Anslinger, also condemned Allentuck and Bowman for publicizing conclusions from such a narrow data base and predicted that the public would be lulled into believing that marihuana was not dangerous.[11] He offered a series of methodological criticisms whose common point was that the LaGuardia Committee's experimental setting did not accurately replicate the naturalistic context of marihuana use and thus distorted the "actual" effects of the drug. Bouquet noted, for example, that the structure of the experiment limited

the amount of marihuana used and restrained the user from out-
landish or dangerous behavior. In a natural setting, Bouquet con-
tended, the user would not so limit his own intake; on the contrary,
he would use to excess. Furthermore, there would be no artificial
constraints on his response, and so he would inevitably turn to
crime. To demonstrate these points, Bouquet referred to the "in-
veterate hemp smokers that one meets in India, the Near East, and
North Africa." This methodological criticism became the mainstay
of the bureau's condemnation of the LaGuardia Report. Excerpts
from Bouquet's letter were reprinted in *Traffic in Opium.*[12]

Bowman replied to Bouquet's letter in June 1944, but he did not
deal with the latter's methodological criticisms, noting that the
imminent release of the LaGuardia Report itself would present his
data in more detail. Instead, he criticized Bouquet's stress upon
the consequences rather than the validity of the research.

It is somewhat surprising to find objection to the publication of carefully
worked out studies on the ground that it is improper and dangerous rather
than to raise the one issue of science—was the study carried out in a proper
scientific manner and are the authors justified in drawing the conclusions
that they did from the studies made?[13]

The publication of the final LaGuardia Report, however, merely
led to more strident criticism. Although it had previously welcomed
the Allentuck-Bowman study, JAMA condemned the final report
in an editorial in April 1945.

For many years medical scientists have considered cannabis a dangerous
drug. Nevertheless, a book called "Marihuana Problem" by the New York
City Mayor's Committee on Marihuana submits an analysis by seventeen
doctors of tests on 77 prisoners and, on this narrow and thoroughly un-
scientific foundation, draws sweeping and inadequate conclusions which
minimize the harmfulness of marihuana.[14]

The editorial went on to cite contrary evidence—a case where a
bellboy under the influence of marihuana killed a federal guard
and a study by Marcovitz and Myers that linked marihuana to
various kinds of psychopathology. It argued that the report would
hinder law enforcement by encouraging use and gave one example
of a youth who cited it as a justification for using the drug.

The editorial, which was reprinted with enthusiastic affirmation by the bureau, brought prompt replies from Walton, who had worked on the pharmacological study, and from Bowman.[15] Both stressed the validity of the data and the moderation of the conclusions. The report, they noted, did acknowledge that marihuana was a problem and did not challenge existing marihuana laws. Bowman weakly noted that critics ignored the pharmacological and sociological studies in favor of the clinical study but did not pursue the implications.

The Walton and Bowman responses, however, did not stop the criticism. Anslinger subsequently wrote a rejoinder that cited studies from India to support his contention that marihuana did lead to crime.[16] Marcovitz joined the debate by arguing that although his own study did not conclude that marihuana caused maladjustment and psychopathology, it did show that marihuana use was an adjunct to these. He criticized the LaGuardia Report again for not looking at use in natural settings, where presumably it would be clearly associated with pathology.[17]

Marcovitz's letter, which appeared in September 1945, was the last installment in the debate over the LaGuardia findings. The whole interchange had been dominated by the bureau. The most obvious indications of this are the lack of challenge to the Marihuana Tax Act or the bureau's enforcement policy and the focus on crime as the major consequence of marihuana use. When we look more closely at the debate, moreover, we find even more striking indications of the bureau's hegemony: the near total neglect of the LaGuardia Committee's sociological study and the fact that JAMA's 1945 editorial probably was written by Anslinger himself.

As we have noted, the bureau's central scientific argument was that the LaGuardia Committee based its conclusions on experimentally observed marihuana use under conditions quite removed from those found in a natural setting. Marihuana users, the bureau maintained, behaved quite differently on the street than they did in experimental settings. No one effectively challenged this argument, despite the fact that its error would have been obvious to anyone who had read the LaGuardia Report. The report's conclusions were not based solely on a clinical study, but on a clinical study *and* a sociological study. The bureau ignored the latter and so did everyone else.

This lacuna was convenient for the bureau because the results of the sociological study defied the simple objections raised against the clinical study. In sending six investigators into tea pads, dance halls, and schoolyards, the LaGuardia Committee did precisely what all its critics condemned it for not doing: It observed marihuana use in a natural setting. Indeed, it was the first to do so. None of the evidence cited by the bureau included observations of the process of marihuana use. What passed for naturalistic study were in fact *post hoc* observations of selected populations of allegedly heavy marihuana users. Since these populations were often in mental hospitals or prisons or just in trouble, it is not surprising that connections between marihuana and pathology were forthcoming.

In contrast, the LaGuardia Committee sent its investigators where everyday marihuana use occurred, and their findings were inconsistent with the dominant marihuana beliefs. In New York City, at least, there was no marihuana traffic in schoolyards and youthful hangouts. The drug was found largely in Harlem and around Broadway. Users were not violent or compulsive: Investigators found that "tea pads" were relaxed, congenial places with virtually no violence or erotic activity. Users generally limited their intake quite carefully, and there was no indication that marihuana use led to hard drug use.[18]

Not only did the dominant reading of the LaGuardia Report conform to the bureau's interests by ignoring the most unpalatable section but the AMA journal itself appears to have capitulated to the bureau at a pivotal moment. Richard Bonnie and Charles Whitebread II have noted that "judging from subsequent collaboration between Anslinger and this Journal," the 1945 JAMA editorial was probably written by Anslinger himself.[19]

There is a wealth of internal evidence to support this claim. To put it simply, the 1945 editorial condemnation of the LaGuardia Report sounds very different from other JAMA writing on marihuana at the time and very similar to the letters from Anslinger and Bouquet. Much of this involves subtle questions of tone and style, but there are a number of straightforward similarities and differences as well. First, the 1945 LaGuardia editorial flatly contradicted the 1942 Allentuck-Bowman editorial, though both reviewed the same clinical study. The earlier piece praised the scientific achievement of the study that the later piece condemned. Second, the 1945 editorial addressed neither the AMA's general concern with the lack of quality data on marihuana nor its interest in furthering research. It did not treat marihuana as an object of scientific knowledge as both the 1942 editorial and Herman Kretsch-mer's 1945 AMA presidential address did.[20] Third, the 1945 editorial did stress themes found in the Anslinger and Bouquet letters. It emphasized the threat of the LaGuardia Report to law enforcement, and it gave examples of marihuana crimes. Moreover, it sounded threatened. The LaGuardia Report, however, did not threaten the interests of the AMA, since it was consistent with the AMA's primary goal of furthering research on marihuana. In contrast, it did threaten the FBN, since it questioned central tenets of the bureau's case against marihuana. The editorial, in short, was written from a law enforcement, not a medical, perspective. Fourth, the 1945 editorial misquoted Kolb's response in the same way as Bouquet had in his 1944 letter. Both pieces cite Kolb as saying, "one may say of such a drug that, if it were abused as alcohol is abused, it might be an important cause of crimes and other misdemeanors." In fact, as noted earlier, Kolb said, "if used as widely as alcohol is used in this country"—quite a different qualification. The assertion, further-more, was taken out of context in the same way by both Bouquet and the JAMA editorial. Taking these bits of evidence together leads to the conclusion that the 1945 editorial bears the unmistakable mark of Anslinger and the bureau.[21]

STEPPING-STONE

In the early 1950s, marihuana continued to be seen as a dangerous drug requiring strict legal controls, but the established claim that marihuana led to violence shared the stage with the stepping-stone hypothesis that marihuana use led to the use of harder drugs, par-ticularly heroin. The introduction of the Stepping-stone Hypothesis was a response to the particular needs of the bureau in the 1950s, perceived changes in use patterns, and the continuing undercurrent of skepticism regarding the dangers of marihuana.

The notion of progression to harder drugs had never been wholly absent from earlier discussions of marihuana. Lewis had mentioned it in his 1913 *Cosmopolitan* short story, and there had been short discussions of it in several articles in the 1930s.[22] Anslinger, however, had explicitly denied such a connection in the 1937 Marihuana Tax Act hearings, and it had never received the attention given to the link between marihuana and violent crime.

The bureau's first reference to the Stepping-stone Hypothesis came in its report for 1949:

The Bureau has noticed during the past few years an alarming increase in the number of young persons . . . arrested for violation of the Federal marihuana and narcotic laws in New York, Chicago, and San Francisco. . . . There also has been an increasing number of these young narcotic offenders who admit starting the use of narcotics with marihuana, then after a short while changing to the more powerful narcotics such as heroin, morphine, and cocaine.[23]

This new claim against marihuana gained commonsense status quickly. Less than two years later, the progression from marihuana to heroin was already regarded as a "tragically familiar story."[24] Periodical articles made it the mainstay of their arguments against marihuana. Four of the six *Readers' Guide* articles between 1949 and 1954 stressed the Stepping-stone Hypothesis, while only three of forty articles in the sample prior to 1949 did so.[25] The articles were often defensive in theme. They stressed that even occasional marihuana use was harmful, despite claims to the contrary. These contrary claims were not identified, but clearly the repercussions of the LaGuardia Report were still being felt: Anslinger made a pointed condemnation of the report at the 1950 congressional hearings on organized crime.[26]

"Bodies and minds can be wrecked by even one 'adventure' taken 'just for the thrill of it'," warned columnist Earl Wilson, who cited both progression and violence as the possible results of experimentation with marihuana. Marihuana may not be addicting, counseled *Science Digest,* but it is still dangerous because "it leads thrill-seekers on to more dangerous drugs." Marihuana *is* more dangerous than alcohol, because "it makes the switch to heroin easy," noted *Newsweek* in 1954 in conclusion to a report on the airing of a promarihuana program on radio station KPFA in Berkeley, California.[27]

The Stepping-stone Hypothesis was no less prevalent during the numerous organized crime, drug control, and juvenile delinquency hearings of the 1950s and early 1960s when marihuana was discussed.[28] Violent crime received markedly less attention. Two passages are particularly important because they shed light on the function performed by the Stepping-stone Hypothesis in the wider discussion of drug control policy. The first comes from the 1951 House of Representatives hearings on drug control in a discussion of barbiturates. Anslinger had argued that barbiturates ought not to be made illegal, and Congressman Boggs was trying to ascertain his reasons. The question arose as to whether or not barbiturates were as dangerous as some currently illegal drugs, particularly marihuana.

Mr. Boggs. Are not [barbiturates] . . . as dangerous as marihuana is?
Mr. Anslinger. I do not think so.
Mr. Boggs. From just what little I saw in that demonstration, I have forgotten the figure Dr. Isbell gave, but my recollection is that only a small percentage of those marihuana cases was anything more than a temporary degree of exhilaration, but those barbiturates pictures indicated to me there is something much worse than that produced by barbiturates.
Mr. Anslinger. The danger is this: Over 50 per cent of those young addicts started on marijuana smoking. They started there and graduated to heroin; they took the needle when the thrill of marijuana was gone. You do not find those young people taking barbiturates and graduating to heroin.[29]

The second passage is found in the 1955 Senate hearings on the illicit narcotics traffic. Anslinger had argued that the bureau's addict census had shown a precipitous drop in the rate of heroin addiction since the 1920s, thus implying that the bureau had done a good job. He then discussed how the census was constructed, particularly what kinds of addicts were included.

Now we are trying to confine this, however, to the nonmedical drug addicts, the addict who buys his drugs in the underworld or obtains drugs by other unlawful means, such as robbing drugstores or forging prescriptions, and *we are trying to keep away from the marihuana addict* [emphasis added], because he is not the true addict. The true addict is the addict to opium derivatives or synthetic narcotic drugs.[30]

Anslinger, in other words, attempted to de-emphasize the dangers of marihuana per se to justify not including marihuana "addicts" in the bureau's census. The reference to marihuana was meant as an aside, but Senator Price Daniel did not let it pass.

Senator Daniel. Now, do I understand it from you that, while we are discussing marihuana, the real danger there is that the use of marihuana leads many people eventually to the use of heroin, and the drugs that do cause them complete addiction; is that true?

Mr. Anslinger. That is the great problem and our great concern about the use of marihuana, that eventually if used over a long period, it does lead to heroin addiction. The marihuana habit, it is a habit-forming drug as distinguished from an addiction-forming drug, is relatively easy to break.

Anslinger not only denied that marihuana was addicting but also omitted any reference to violent crime or any other danger tied directly to marihuana. Senators Daniel and Herman Welker, no doubt recalling earlier assertions about marihuana crime, asked Anslinger whether or not marihuana caused the user to "commit crimes and do many heinous things." Anslinger answered yes but seemed unwilling to elaborate. He gave no rendition of marihuana crimes and even de-emphasized the importance of the crime connection: "There have been many brutal crimes traced to marihuana, but I would not say that it is the controlling factor in the commission of crimes."

Why did the Stepping-stone Hypothesis become central to discussions of marihuana control policy in the 1950s? The discussion so far gives some clues, and there are others. Its rise reflects both a perceived shift in heroin users and a change in the bureau's structural needs.

In the late 1940s, the average age of the heroin user seemed to be declining. At the 1937 Senate hearings on the Marihuana Tax Act, Anslinger had assured the assembled senators that the marihuana user was quite different from the opiate user: The former was generally in his teens or twenties, while the latter was about thirty-five or forty. In 1949, however, the median age of those admitted to the federal narcotics hospitals for heroin addiction showed a significant drop; the marihuana user and heroin user suddenly appeared to be drawn from the same age group.[31] This data made it plausible that marihuana use was somehow connected to heroin use, a notion corroborated by the testimony of heroin users themselves, at least some of whom claimed to have started with marihuana.

Whatever we make of the Stepping-stone Hypothesis, the underlying notion of confluence seems plausible. Indeed, it may have been an unintended consequence of the bureau's own enforcement activity and of World War II. In the 1930s, marihuana and heroin were used by different groups and distributed separately. Most marihuana was grown domestically and sold in an unorganized fashion, while most heroin was illegally imported by an organized smuggling network. With passage of the Marihuana Tax Act, the bureau began to supervise large-scale eradication of the illicit domestic hemp crop.[32] In the early 1940s, the war obstructed the international heroin trade.[33] With the supply of heroin cut off and with an un-fulfilled demand for marihuana, organized smugglers began im-porting the latter on a large scale. This is reflected in the FBN reports for 1944, which noted an upsurge in the organized illicit traffic, and for 1945, which reported for the first time that border seizures of marihuana exceeded domestic seizures. When the heroin trade resumed after the war, marihuana and heroin became available from the same sources. This may have increased the probability that persons who used one drug would also use the other.

The rise of the Stepping-stone Hypothesis, in short, was con-sistent with demographic changes in drug use as these were per-ceived by the bureau and other policymakers. This is probably not the whole story, however. The Stepping-stone Hypothesis also may have served the interests of the bureau by allowing it to justify continued controls over marihuana despite skepticism about the drug's dangers, to oppose controls over barbiturates, and to exclude marihuana "addicts" from the bureau's census. We can look at each of these possibilities in turn.

To justify its continued jurisdiction over marihuana, the bureau had to demonstrate that the drug was indeed dangerous. Ques-tions about the immediate dangers of use, however, had not been quieted by the bureau's condemnation of the LaGuardia Report in the mid-1940s. There remained an undercurrent of dissent, which surfaced just enough to make the bureau wary. In the organized crime hearings in 1950, for example, Harris Isbell, the director of the Lexington narcotics hospital, testified that "marijuana users generally are mildly intoxicated, giggle, laugh, bother no one, and have a good time."[34] He questioned the links between marihuana and violent crime, sexual immorality, and addiction, conceding only that marihuana might precipitate a temporary psychosis in "predisposed individuals" and could lead to the use of harder drugs. The Stepping-stone Hypothesis spared the bureau the unseemly task of continually responding to critics by allowing it to argue that although marihuana use might be innocuous enough in itself, it led to heroin use, which was unquestionably dangerous. Once the hypothesis had become accepted, moreover, the very harmlessness of marihuana became an argument against its use. For example, Victor Vogel of Lexington testified that young persons who had used marihuana readily took up heroin because their marihuana experience convinced them that narcotics in general were nonaddicting.[35]

The bureau's need to provide an unquestionable picture of the dangers of marihuana use was made particularly urgent by pressure for barbiturate control. On three separate occasions, congressmen, responding to considerable popular pressure, suggested making barbiturates illegal.[36] In return, the resolute reticence of the bureau asserted itself again: Anslinger passionately rejected the proposal each time, arguing that barbiturate prohibition would be widely unpopular, would antagonize powerful medical and pharmaceutical interests, would ultimately be unenforceable, and would drag his small bureau into disrepute. He would have none of it. To justify his refusal, Anslinger had to argue that barbiturates were less dangerous than illegal drugs. The Stepping-stone Hypothesis allowed him to do so unambiguously with marihuana by linking it with heroin, which was unanimously believed to be worse than barbiturates.

At the same time that the bureau refused jurisdiction over barbiturates, it buttressed its request for extended powers over narcotics by using the low addict census count to prove that it was using its existing powers successfully. To maintain as low a count as possible, it needed a reason for excluding marihuana users from the census. The Stepping-stone Hypothesis allowed the bureau to argue that although marihuana was dangerous and thus properly illegal (since it led to heroin use), marihuana users in themselves were not a problem (since they became a problem only when they became heroin users) and hence did not have to be included in an addict count.

DEMISE OF THE CONSENSUS

The bureau's consensus on the dangers of marihuana and the propriety of harsh penalties remained intact until the late 1950s and early 1960s. At that time, public health officials and others began to make their dissent heard. Not only did they express their doubts about the dangers of marihuana more loudly but they also challenged the penalties themselves. The dissenters ultimately found a forum in the various official inquiries into drug abuse sponsored by President John F. Kennedy.

The immediate cause of the upsurge in dissent may well have been the bureau's success in securing the harsh drug controls that it had wanted. At its behest, Congress had passed the Boggs Act of 1951 and the Narcotic Control Act of 1956, which greatly increased the penalties for drug offenses. By 1957 possession of marihuana carried a minimum sentence of two years for the first offense, five for the second, and ten for the third. First and second trafficking offenses entailed minimum sentences of five and ten years respectively. With the exception of a first possession offense, all convictions carried a mandatory sentence with no chance of parole or probation. The penalty schedule for marihuana was made exactly the same as that for opiates and cocaine.[37]

For those who regarded marihuana as relatively innocuous, the increased penalties appeared absurd, and the absurdity made them speak up. Some of the first cries of dissent were heard at the 1958 symposium on the history of narcotic drug addiction problems, sponsored by the National Institute of Mental Health. Dr. Harris Isbell conceded the potential danger of marihuana but still questioned the penalties:

Marihuana is undoubtedly a potentially harmful intoxicant, but there is no sense in sending a person to the penitentiary for 10 years for having one marihuana cigarette in his pocket, a cigarette that would surely have no more effect on him than one drink of whiskey. Such treatment is ridiculous, fantastic, and a disgrace to our civilization.[38]

Judge Edward J. Dimock expressed similar sentiments:

I don't think that I am entirely unreasonable in objecting to the necessity of having to send a hare-brained saxophone player away for 10 years for having a pack of marihuana cigarettes in his pocket.[39]

The notions that marihuana was less dangerous than commonly believed and that marihuana controls were much too harsh—both anathema to the bureau—received considerable legitimacy from President Kennedy's drug abuse committees. Both the Ad Hoc Panel on Drug Abuse in 1962 and the Advisory Commission on

Narcotic and Drug Abuse in 1963 tersely questioned the existing penalties.

It is the opinion of the Panel that the hazards of marihuana *per se* have been exaggerated and that long criminal sentences imposed on an occasional user or possessor of the drug are in poor social perspective.[40]

The present federal narcotics and marihuana laws equate the two drugs. . . . In most cases [however] the marihuana reefer is less harmful than any opiate. For one thing, while marihuana may provoke lawless behavior, it does not create physical dependence. This Commission makes a flat distinction between the two drugs and believes that the unlawful sale or possession of marihuana is a less serious offense than the unlawful sale or possession of an opiate.[41]

Here, then, were the first major challenges to the bureau's marihuana consensus since it was established in the 1930s. To be sure, the effect was largely symbolic. There was no rush to reduce marihuana penalties and no sense of urgency. Only after there was an increase in middle-class marihuana use did the issue of penalty reduction become an urgent one. Nevertheless, the reports of the panel and the commission marked the end of the simple days during which the FBN with its image of marihuana as a "killer weed" and a stepping-stone to heroin had totally dominated the formation of marihuana policy.[42] At the same time, they opened the way for a new set of marihuana beliefs that would be shaped by the events of the 1960s.

MARIHUANA BEFORE THE SIXTIES: A SUMMARY

The Bureau and Marihuana

Once it decided to take up the marihuana issue, the Federal Bureau of Narcotics decisively shaped public discussion and the law for over two-and-a-half decades. It dominated the marihuana hearings of 1937 and created the marihuana consensus of the late 1930s. The bureau was able to discredit the LaGuardia Report in the 1940s by making the American Medical Association withdraw its editorial approval and by defining how the report was discussed. Finally, when it introduced the Stepping-stone Hypothesis in the early 1950s, the claim, which appears to have reflected the bureau's own interests, quickly came to dominate discussions of marihuana.

The bureau, however, did not spontaneously seek jurisdiction over marihuana. Contrary to the popular view, it did not consistently attempt to legislate morality or to expand its purview. Chastened by the failure of Prohibition, the court challenges to the Harrison Act, and the budgetary restrictions of the Depression, it explicitly downplayed the marihuana issue in the early 1930s and attempted to have the states deal with the drug. The bureau's main effort thus went into procuring adoption and state passage of the Uniform Narcotic Drugs Act. Its decision to seek a national marihuana law arose in a round-about way from its propaganda campaign on behalf of the Uniform Narcotic Drug Act and paradoxically was an unintended consequence of its attempt to avoid immediate national legislation.

The bureau, in short, developed a strategy of resolute reticence to survive in an unsupportive environment. It sought to protect itself by avoiding additional enforcement responsibilities where it could. This strategy was manifest not only in its treatment of marihuana in the early 1930s but also in its categorical refusal to accept barbiturate control in the early 1950s. To understand the bureau, then, we must see both its faces—the aggressive way it fought to maintain the authority it could not avoid and its aversion to extending that authority.

The bureau's success in dominating public discussion of marihuana, moreover, rested on specific social conditions. The bureau succeeded because marihuana use prior to the 1960s was an insignificant issue, because no other organized groups had an interest in the fate of the drug, and because its users were socially marginal and few in number. Hardly anyone knew about marihuana or had an interest in it. The populace at large hardly knew its name; there were few sources of information other than the bureau; and the declining medical use of the drug by the 1930s gave manufacturers, physicians, and pharmacists only a token interest in opposing the bureau's propaganda. In such circumstances, the bureau could shape the image of marihuana with minimal effort and with little likelihood of opposition or rebuttal. The paucity and marginality of the users, moreover, made it unlikely that otherwise reputable citizens would be arrested, that nonusers would have any firsthand experience with users, or that the users themselves would effectively organize. The bureau's hegemony thus was not disturbed by other interest groups, organized users, or a concerned general public. In the late 1960s, all this would change.

Mexicans and Marihuana

Political pressure motivated by anti-Mexican sentiment in the Southwest does not appear to have played an important role in the passage of the Marihuana Tax Act. The bureau had no trouble resisting the local political pressure that it felt in the early 1930s— whatever its source. More importantly, references to Mexican users virtually disappeared from discussions of marihuana in the mid-1930s, and the bureau's propaganda for the Marihuana Tax Act stressed the peril to youth. Had the act been primarily an effort to placate the Southwest's concern about Mexicans, one would have expected the bureau to play up the evils of that group's use.

The association of marihuana with Mexican laborers and other lower-class groups, however, affected beliefs and policy in a more subtle, though no less significant, way. The image of marihuana that became dominant in the mid-1930s was shaped indirectly by stereotypes of these groups. Because Mexican laborers and the others were socially marginal and disreputable, marihuana was perceived as alien to the mainstream of society, and its alleged spread to youth was seen as "infection." More importantly, because these groups were typified as violent, marihuana became seen as a "killer weed." The images of "infection" and "killer weed" in turn were used to justify antimarihuana legislation. In short, the mediating link between Mexicans and the Marihuana Tax Act was a particular conception of marihuana.

The Killer Weed

Marihuana thus became known as a "killer weed" for two reasons. The first was the initial social locus of drug use: Marihuana became known as a drug that produced violence because initially it was associated with Mexicans and other lower-class groups. This image of marihuana developed in the Southwest and New Orleans in the 1910s and 1920s and was transmitted by local officials and narcotics agents to the relevant authorities in the federal government. The second reason was the entrepreneurship of the Federal Bureau of Narcotics, which popularized the "killer weed" image in the process of securing state and federal drug control legislation in the 1930s.

Once established, the image persisted partly because of continued FBN publicity, partly because of inertia: The more the claim was repeated, the more it was likely to be repeated, until significant social changes rendered the old image obsolete and created a new image to replace it.

The violence claim was joined in the 1950s by the assertion that marihuana was a stepping-stone to heroin, but it would not be supplanted until the 1960s when the kind of danger imputed to the drug would change dramatically.

NOTES

1. U.S., Federal Bureau of Narcotics, *Traffic in Opium and Other Dangerous Drugs* (Washington, D.C.: U.S. Government Printing Office, 1938), pp. 45-46. The bureau's annual reports are identified by the year they cover, not the year of publication. See also ibid., 1937, pp. 53-54; 1939, pp. 54-55, 59; 1940, p. 49. The lack of large-scale illicit trafficking in marihuana was used in the early 1930s to justify federal nonintervention on the grounds that the problem was outside federal jurisdiction (ibid., 1931, pp. 51-52). By the late 1930s, the same condition was claimed to be the result of timely federal intervention and thus used to justify that intervention.

2. Ibid., 1939, p. 15.

3. Robert P. Walton, "The Marihuana Problem," *Science,* 25 May 1945, pp. 538-539; "Menace of Marihuana," *Science Digest,* July 1945, pp. 49-50; "The Weed," *Time,* 19 July 1943, pp. 54-56. There were eleven articles in all in the *Readers' Guide* sample between 1941 and 1948, but three did not address the issue of danger. Although none of the eleven articles challenged the illegality of marihuana, two other sources did. In 1943, J. M. Phalen, editor of the *Military Surgeon,* argued that marihuana was no more dangerous than tobacco and that antimarihuana laws were ill-advised. Phalen's comments and the findings of the 1894 Indian Hemp Commission were cited in 1949 by Norman Taylor to make a similar case against marihuana laws. See Norman Taylor, *Flight from Reality* (New York: Duell, Sloan, and Pearce, 1949), pp. 21-43.

4. "Marihuana Found Useful in Certain Ills," *Science News Letter,* 30 May 1942, p. 341; Walton, "Marihuana Problem"; "What Happens to

Marihuana Smokers," *Science Digest,* May 1945, pp. 35-40; "Menace of Marihuana," *Science Digest.*

5. David Solomon, ed., *The Marihuana Papers* (New York: New American Library, 1966), p. 280. The LaGuardia Report is reprinted with some lengthy methodological sections removed in Solomon, pp. 279-410.

6. Samuel Allentuck and Karl Bowman, "The Psychiatric Aspects of Marihuana Intoxication," *American Journal of Psychiatry* 99 (1942): 248-250.

7. Lawrence Kolb, "Discussion," *American Journal of Psychiatry* 99 (1942):251.

8. *Journal of the American Medical Association (JAMA)* 120 (1942): 1128-1129.

9. *JAMA* 121 (1943):212-213.

10. Anslinger's handling of data was also interesting in other ways. First, his ambivalence toward prisoner studies, originally noted in the differential treatment of Stanley and Bromberg, continued. The Allentuck-Bowman study was methodologically sound when it supported the bureau but unsound when it did not. Second, in his long list of citations, he quoted the Indian Hemp Commission as saying that marihuana use causes insanity—an assertion that is hardly representative of the commission's conclusions.

11. Letter to the editor, *JAMA* 124 (1944):1010-1011.

12. Federal Bureau of Narcotics, *Traffic,* 1943, pp. 7-9.

13. *JAMA* 125 (1944):376.

14. *JAMA* 127 (1945):1129.

15. Bureau of Narcotics, *Traffic,* 1945, p. 11; *JAMA* 128 (1945): 383, 899-900.

16. *JAMA* 128 (1945):1187.

17. *JAMA* 129 (1945):378. Marcovitz and Myers studied thirty-five confirmed marihuana users in the U.S. Army and found them to be generally maladjusted, alienated, rebellious against authority, unwilling to work, and so forth. They showed histories of crime and adverse family and economic conditions.

18. Solomon, *Marihuana Papers,* pp. 292-307.

19. Richard Bonnie and Charles Whitebread II, *The Marihuana Conviction* (Charlottesville: University of Virginia Press, 1974), p. 201.

20. *JAMA* 129 (1945):1105-1109.

21. How the Bureau was able to control so decisively the AMA's official stance on marihuana is unclear. I merely wish to show that it did.

22. Alfred H. Lewis, "Marihuana," *Cosmopolitan,* October 1913, pp. 645-655; Frank Gomila and Madeline Lambou, "Present Status of the Marihuana Vice in the United States," in *Marihuana,* ed. Robert P. Walton (Philadelphia: J. B. Lippincott, 1938), pp. 27-39; Earl Rowell and Robert

Rowell, *On the Trail of Marihuana: The Weed of Madness* (Mountain View, Calif.: Pacific Press, 1939).
23. Bureau of Narcotics, *Traffic*, 1949, pp. 6-7.
24. U.S., House of Representatives, Committee on Ways and Means, *Control of Narcotics, Marijuana, Barbiturates*, 82d Cong., 1st sess., 1951, p. 40.
25. The four articles were Earl Wilson, "Crazy Dreamers," *Collier's*, 4 June 1949, pp. 27-32; "Saw-toothed," *New Yorker*, 11 August 1951, pp. 18-19; "Wicked Weed," *Science Digest*, April 1952, p. 48; and "Reefers on KPFA," *Newsweek*, 10 May 1954, p. 92. The other two articles—one a report of marihuana cultivation in window boxes ("Marihuana may lurk in window boxes," *Science News Letter*, 28 July 1951, p. 60) and the other a story on use by Marines at Camp Pendleton ("Marines and marihuana," *Newsweek*, 31 December 1951, p. 17)—did not discuss the effects of marihuana. Only one article (Wilson, "Crazy Dreamers") paid attention to violence.
26. U.S., Senate, Special Committee to Investigate Organized Crime in Interstate Commerce, *Organized Crime in Interstate Commerce*, 81st Cong., 2d sess., 1950, p. 427.
27. Wilson, "Crazy Dreamers"; "Wicked Weed," *Science Digest;* "Reefers," *Newsweek.*
28. Senate, *Organized Crime*, pp. 119-120, 139-150, 261-271, 448-462; House of Representatives, *Control of Narcotics*, pp. 100, 105, 107, 206; U.S., Senate, Committee on the Judiciary, Subcommittee on Improvements in the Federal Criminal Code, *Illicit Narcotics Traffic*, 84th Cong., 1955, pp. 16-18; U.S., House of Representatives, Committee on Ways and Means, *Traffic in, and Control of, Narcotics, Barbiturates, and Amphetamines*, 84th Cong., 1956, pp. 196, 814-815, 1062-1063; U.S., Senate, Committee on the Judiciary, Subcommittee to Investigate Juvenile Delinquency, *Juvenile Delinquency*, 86th Cong., 2d sess., 87th Cong., 2d sess., 1960-1962, pp. 595, 1104-1110; U.S., Senate, Committee on Government Operations, *Organized Crime and Illicit Traffic in Narcotics*, 88th Cong., 1963, pp. 694-695, 700, 746.
29. House of Representatives, *Control of Narcotics*, p. 206.
30. Senate, *Illicit Narcotics Traffic*, pp. 16-18.
31. Bureau of Narcotics, *Traffic*, 1949, pp. 6-7; House of Representatives, *Control of Narcotics*, p. 44.
32. Bureau of Narcotics, *Traffic*, 1937, p. 53.
33. Alfred McCoy, *The Politics of Heroin in Southeast Asia* (New York: Harper and Row, 1973).
34. Senate, *Organized Crime*, pp. 119-120.
35. Ibid., p. 244.

36. Ibid., pp. 429-432; House of Representatives, *Control of Narcotics,* pp. 73, 204-206; House of Representatives, *Traffic in, and Control of, Narcotics,* pp. 191-196.

37. Alfred Lindesmith, *The Addict and the Law* (New York: Random House, 1965), p. 26.

38. Robert B. Livingston, ed., *History of Narcotic Drug Addiction Problems* (Washington, D.C.: Public Health Service, 1958), p. 47.

39. Ibid., p. 144.

40. U.S., President's Ad Hoc Panel on Drug Abuse, *Progress Report* (Washington, D.C.: U.S. Government Printing Office, 1962), p. 286.

41. U.S., President's Advisory Commission on Narcotic and Drug Abuse, *Final Report* (Washington, D.C.: U.S. Government Printing Office, 1963), p. 42.

42. The advisory commission challenged the dominance of the bureau in other ways as well. First, its very existence indicated growing White House concern with drug control policy and thus a preemption of the bureau's monopoly of the area. Second, the commission recommended both the repeal of major sections of the Boggs and Narcotic Control acts and a major reorganization of federal drug control.

THE
EMBOURGEOISEMENT OF
MARIHUANA

6

Public perceptions of the dangers of marihuana use and legal penalties against the drug changed dramatically in the United States in the late 1960s and early 1970s. Prior to that time, as we have just seen, marihuana had been widely condemned as a dangerous drug; the application of criminal sanctions against the user had been generally approved; and by the late 1950s, the penalties had become quite harsh. Beginning in the mid-1960s, however, the consensus that marihuana was an inherently dangerous drug broke down; the appropriateness of criminal sanctions against the user was broadly questioned; and penalties for use were significantly reduced. Marihuana use did not become wholly socially acceptable, but it was at least partially domesticated.

It has been common to explain these changes as the results of the large-scale spread of marihuana use to what are colloquially called "middle-class" youth—the offspring of the professional, managerial, and business strata, the affluent and the rich, and the college-educated. We have called this the Embourgeoisement Hypothesis. The demographic shift in use to middle-class youth was well under way by the mid-1960s, and both public officials and the media were quick to perceive it. As we have noted, the first magazine articles on the topic appeared in 1964 and 1965. By 1966 the concern about youthful drug use that was perennially voiced in congressional drug hearings had been joined by a more specific worry over youthful middle-class marihuana use.[1] The observation that middle-class youth were the major and typical users of marihuana became a commonplace. Epidemiologist Lillian Blackford (whose yearly surveys of drug use became a mainstay of the literature), for example, made the following pointed assessment of drug use in suburban San Mateo County in California:

In 1966 it became painfully apparent that San Mateo County had developed a drug problem among young people. In the ten years from 1956 through 1965 there had been 45 juvenile drug referrals, generally concerned with hard narcotics and stemming from our small black and Mexican population. In 1966 there were 157 referrals, many of which were concerned with marihuana and definitely from more privileged youngsters.[2]

The important question is how precisely the changed social background of marihuana users brought about the concomitant changes in the perceptions of the drug's dangers and in the laws concerning its use. The answer lies partly in the new social interests mobilized within the drug control arena. The spread of marihuana use to middle-class youth gave these youth and their parents, including the policymakers themselves, a direct interest in reforming marihuana laws and thus injected a powerful new force into the drug control debate. At the same time, however, the shift in use altered the entire ideological framework within which that debate took place, in effect transforming the very structure of the drug control arena. The terms in which marihuana users and the law were discussed by nearly everyone changed substantially.

There are, in short, at least two different ways of looking at the impact of the social background of the marihuana user on public perceptions of the drug and on the state of the law—one that looks at the organized interests attempting to shape the law and another that examines the ideological framework within which the law was discussed. We shall present a model that incorporates both. Before doing so, however, let us take a closer look at how both public perceptions and the law actually changed. In the conservative days of the early 1980s, it is tempting to minimize the extent to which the societal response to marihuana has changed in the last fifteen years. Marihuana is still far from full social acceptability; the arrest rate

for use remains high (over 400,000 a year); and widespread debate
about the dangers of the drug continues. The election of President
Ronald Reagan and the emergence of the New Right, moreover,
augur poorly for further marihuana law reform. Despite all this,
both the marihuana laws and the assessments of the dangers of the
drug changed sharply in the late 1960s and early 1970s.

REASSESSING THE DANGERS

Despite some demurral, prior to 1964 marihuana generally was
regarded as a dangerous drug. In the mid-1960s, this easy consensus
gave way to large-scale debate and to a cacophony of opinion ranging
from outright praise for the drug to dire warnings about a "marihuana-hashish" epidemic. Beat poet Allen Ginsberg expressed one
extreme in his 1966 *Atlantic Monthly* article.

How much there is to be revealed about marihuana in this decade in America
for the general public. . . . The marijuana consciousness is one that, ever
so gently, shifts the center of attention from habitual shallow, purely verbal
guidelines and repetitive second-hand ideological interpretations of experience to more direct, slower, absorbing, occasionally microscopically minute
engagement with sensing phenomena.[3]

Some eight years later, Senator James O. Eastland voiced the other
extreme in an introduction to his marihuana-hashish hearings.

I consider the hearings which are the subject of this record to be among
the most significant ever held . . . by any committee of Congress. . . .
They may play a role in reversing a trend towards national disaster. Without
public awareness, our country has become caught up in a marihuana-hashish
epidemic that probably eclipses, in gravity, the national epidemics that
have had so debilitating an effect on the population of a number of Middle
Eastern countries.[4]

In between there were many who showed the measured concern of
a 1965 *Time* article, which found marihuana "something to be concerned about" but not "to panic over,"[5] or the guarded approval
of Dr. Joel Fort, who regarded it as a relatively harmless drug but
rejected the "turn on, tune in, drop out mystique."[6]
    The predominant opinion in the 1964-1976 period held that the

dangers of marihuana had been greatly exaggerated in previous years and that the drug was generally a mild "hallucinogen," "intoxicant," or "euphoriant," not a dangerous narcotic.[7] In the *Readers' Guide* sample, 57 percent of the articles from 1964-1976 pictured marihuana as "not-so-dangerous," as compared to 23 percent from 1890-1963 and only 5 percent from 1935-1940, the period of the Federal Bureau of Narcotics's greatest antimarihuana publicity (see Table 8). Even the conservative *National Review* agreed with "the growing speculation in medical circles that cannabis may be no more dangerous than tobacco or liquor."[8]

Table 8
DEGREE OF DANGER, 1964-1976
(Total N = 59)

Time Period	Articles regarding marihuana as:		
	Dangerous	*Not So Dangerous*	*Relevant N*[a]
1964-1976	19 (43%)	25 (57%)	44 (100%)
1890-1963	34 (77%)	10 (23%)	44 (100%)
1935-1940	20 (95%)	1 (5%)	21 (100%)

1890-1963 *vs.* 1964-1976   Corrected Chi Square[b]= 9.3   p<.01
1935-1940 *vs.* 1964-1976   Corrected Chi Square = 14.0   p<.001

[a]Relevant N refers to the total number of articles discussing the danger issue.
[b]All chi squares are calculated using Yates's correction.

More importantly, a broad consensus emerged that moderate, nonproblematic use was possible. Users were deemed capable of limiting their use in order to avoid whatever major harmful effects marihuana might have. For the first time, the "social" or "experimental" user was widely distinguished from the heavy, "problem" user.[9] Pediatrician Benjamin Spock, for example, counseled parents not to worry about occasional use.

I wouldn't be seriously shocked or disillusioned if I [discovered] . . . that my adolescent child . . . had gone against my advice and tried marijuana once, or even occasionally. In today's drug climate that wouldn't mean to me that he was a pot head or a delinquent.[10]

In all, 80 percent of the articles that dealt with the issue allowed for the possibility of some moderate use as compared to 44 percent in the entire 1890-1963 period and 27 percent in the late 1930s (see Table 9).

Table 9
POSSIBILITY OF MODERATE USE, 1964-1976
(Total N = 59)

Articles regarding moderate use as:

Time Period	Possible	Impossible	Relevant N[a]
1964-1976	24 (80%)	6 (20%)	30 (100%)
1890-1963	15 (44%)	19 (56%)	34 (100%)
1935-1940	4 (27%)	11 (73%)	15 (100%)

1890-1963 *vs.* 1964-1976   Corrected Chi Square[b]= 7.2 p <.01
1935-1940 *vs.* 1964-1976   Corrected Chi Square = 9.9 p<.01

[a]Relevant N refers to the total number of articles discussing moderate use.
[b]All chi squares are calculated using Yates's correction.

Although hardly any policymakers advocated marihuana use, the tendency to downplay the dangers of marihuana and to recognize the possibility of moderate use also marked major federal drug reports and most congressional hearings. In its task force report on narcotics and drug abuse, the Commission on Law Enforcement and Administration of Justice described marihuana as a "mild hallucinogen" and argued that the risks of marihuana use were no greater than alcohol.[11] While noting that marihuana use was far from totally innocuous, the National Commission on Marihuana and Drug Abuse reached the following conclusion in its 1972 report:

From what is now known about the effects of marihuana, its use at the present level does not constitute a major threat to public health. . . . We believe that experimental or intermittent use of this drug carries minimal risk to the public health and should not be given overzealous attention.[12]

During the various congressional hearings on the 1970 Comprehensive Drug Abuse Prevention and Control Act, the period's major piece of drug control legislation, there was a consensus—shared by nearly everyone except the Liberty Lobby, the American Legion, and Mayor Yorty of Los Angeles—that whatever the potential harm of heavy marihuana use, controlled moderate use with minimal ill effect was possible.[13] This change in the evaluation of marihuana occurred despite the protestations of federal narcotics officials. Although they continued to declaim the dangers of marihuana, particularly in the late 1960s, they no longer dominated public debate as they had previously.[14]

The recognition of moderate use moved marihuana a considerable distance from "hard narcotics," any use of which commonly has been regarded as abusive and dangerous, and brought it closer to drugs like alcohol, the potential dangers of which are regarded as avoidable if it is used "responsibly" and "in moderation."[15] The shift in characterization is important. Even the most dangerous drugs may gain a modicum of social acceptability if their excessive or harmful use can be seen as distinguishable from moderate, harmless use.

In short, not only did marihuana become seen in the 1960s and 1970s as less dangerous than previously supposed, but also the nature of the danger was reconceptualized. Once marihuana ceased to be seen as a "narcotic" and once "moderate" use was recognized, the dangers of the drug were less likely to be seen as total, penetrating, and inevitable. The ultimate fruit of this shift was not a belief that marihuana was harmless but a willingness to regard its dangers as limited, avoidable, and hence within the individual user's control.

THE ROAD TO DECRIMINALIZATION

As of 1965, marihuana laws still bore the mark of the harsh legislation of the 1950s. Simple possession carried penalties of two years for the first offense, five for the second, and ten for the third. Except for the first possession offense, all convictions carried a mandatory sentence with no chance for parole or probation.

The late 1960s and early 1970s, in contrast, witnessed a significant reduction in these penalties. As a first step, a 1966 amendment to the federal law made marihuana violators eligible for parole. Four years later, the major federal penalty reductions were promulgated in the Comprehensive Drug Abuse Prevention and Control Act. Marihuana was separated from "narcotic" drugs and reclassified as a hallucinogen; both simple possession and nonprofit distribution of small amounts were reduced from felonies to misdemeanors; and provision was made for the "conditional discharge" and the expunction of the criminal records of first-offender possessors. The last of these reforms was particularly significant because it provided a way of reducing substantially the stigma of a marihuana conviction. A first-time possession offense literally would leave no mark; for most purposes, it could be treated as if it had never occurred.[16]

During the congressional hearings on the 1970 act, support for penalty reductions of some kind was almost universal, though there was disagreement over how much. Even federal narcotics officials (now housed in the Bureau of Narcotics and Dangerous Drugs within the Justice Department), who had firmly opposed any major mitigation in penalties two years before, agreed that harsh penalties did not work and advocated the significant changes that became embodied in the 1970 act.[17] They were joined by the House Select Committee on Crime whose own hearings had stressed the dangers of marihuana.

The major elements of the 1970 act were copied by most states either directly or through the Uniform Controlled Substances Act, which was based on the federal law. By 1974, virtually all states had reduced possession of marihuana from a felony to a misdemeanor.[18]

In 1972, the National Commission on Marihuana and Drug Abuse went beyond penalty reduction to decriminalization. It recommended that the possession of marihuana for personal use and nonprofit distribution should be decriminalized. It also urged that public use and distribution of small amounts be punishable by a mere fine.[19] By 1978, eleven states with over one-third of the nation's population (Oregon, Alaska, Maine, Colorado, California, Ohio, Minnesota, Mississippi, Nebraska, New York, and North Carolina) had decriminalized marihuana, and a similar change had been formally advocated by President Jimmy Carter on the federal level.[20]

Although decriminalization drew substantial opposition, it also enjoyed widespread support. The commission's proposal was endorsed by a long list of newspapers and by numerous organizations, including the American Bar Association, American Medical Association, American Public Health Association, National Education

Association, Consumers Union, National Council of Churches, National Conference of Commissioners on Uniform State Laws, and American Academy of Pediatrics.[21]

Support for decriminalization, moreover, surfaced in odd places. As early as 1968, Antoni Gollan urged the conservative readership of the *National Review* to reevaluate the criminalization of marihuana use, arguing that the drug was not particularly dangerous and that its use was not an ideological issue. Gollan's article was followed by a rebuttal, but letters in subsequent issues were overwhelmingly favorable. The case for decriminalization was reiterated in 1972 by Richard Cowan, who stressed that support for marihuana penalties ran counter to the conservative grain: "The hysterical myths about marihuana . . . have led conservatives to condone massive programs of social engineering, interference in the affairs of individuals, monstrous bureaucratic waste." Conservative columnists William F. Buckley, Jr., and James J. Kilpatrick added their support, the former openly admitting that he had once used the drug on his yacht in international waters.[22]

Most importantly, a striking consensus developed even among opponents of decriminalization. Marihuana users, nearly everyone agreed, should not be imprisoned for their offense. In other words, those who did not support *de jure* decriminalization usually supported a *de facto* decriminalization. They wanted the law to remain, but the penalties not to be applied. At Senator Eastland's 1974 hearings on the "marihuana-hashish epidemic," for example, despite the voluminous lurid testimony on the evils of the drug and the unanimous opposition to *de jure* decriminalization, no one advocated punishing the user or returning to the penalties of bygone days. Instead, there was a preference for a *de facto* decriminalization. David Martin, senior analyst for the subcommittee, put the matter as follows:

I think [decriminalization] is something upon which just about everyone agrees and very few young people . . . are being sent to jail today for simple possession. But there are some who argue that a . . . minimal penalty should be retained in order to make it clear to young people that society has to protect itself against this, and society does not approve of its use.[23]

In other words, criminal penalties should be kept as a symbolic disapproval of marihuana use, but they should not actually be used against any marihuana users.

In summary, despite the widespread disagreement over marihuana in the late 1960s and early 1970s, a certain consensus came to dominate public discussion. The dangers of marihuana were regarded as limited, and the possibility of moderate use was accepted. Penalty reductions of some kind enjoyed broad support. The notion that no one should go to prison simply for using marihuana insinuated itself into public discussion. A limited social space thus was carved out for marihuana.

MARIHUANA AND MIDDLE-CLASS YOUTH

The spread of marihuana to middle-class youth meant that the average socioeconomic position of late 1960s, early 1970s marihuana users was significantly higher than that of previous users of marihuana and narcotics. This had three important ramifications. First, youthful middle-class users were relatively powerful. Although they did not decisively shape policy, they did put together an organized, educated, vociferous constituency that commanded significant attention. Second, the users were respectable. Independent of any action they took, their middle-class position gave them a relatively high status honor. Third, they were relatively accessible to policy-makers and writers. For the first time, the latter had direct contact with possible marihuana users and thus had an opportunity to see them as total human beings, not merely drug users.

These three components of the marihuana users' middle-class position combined in numerous ways to influence perceptions of the drug and attitudes toward the law. The changes in users' social position systematically altered perceptions of the user (*qua* user), the arrangement of political forces in the marihuana control arena, and the arguments made about the legitimacy of marihuana laws (see Figure 1).

Perceptions of the User

In the late 1960s, several new themes emerged in public discussion of marihuana users, including what we may call *kinship, empathy,* and *normality*. Each in effect constituted a new lens through which use and user were perceived. Each made public discussion more open to positive information on the safety of marihuana use.

Figure 1
THE MIDDLE CLASS AND MARIHUANA

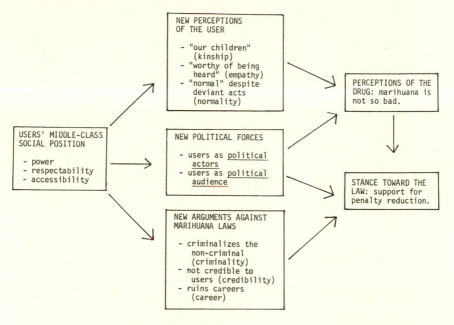

Kinship. With the upsurge of marihuana use among middle-class youth, the enforcement of marihuana laws began to have a direct impact on middle-class families and on policymakers and writers themselves, for it was their sons and daughters who were being arrested and threatened with possible felony convictions for the use or sale of marihuana. Arrests of the offspring of the famous and near-famous became so common that William F. Buckley, Jr., was led to quip: "If the sons of Ethel Kennedy and Sargent Shriver are caught smoking pot why should it surprise us if the son of Francis of Assisi smokes pot?"[24]

An element of self-interest was thus injected into the public discussion of marihuana. Support for decriminalization sometimes arose directly from having one's son or daughter arrested on marihuana charges. At the 1975 Senate hearings on decriminalization, for example, Senator Philip Hart gave this terse reason for supporting the removal of criminal penalties from marihuana possession:

My education, like a lot of people of my generation, included the fact that one of my children is one of the statistics that you have here. He is a minor and spent 20 days in jail for a stub that big [indicating] [brackets in original]. That is all the education I needed to convince me that it—marihuana prosecution policy—was a topsy-turvy operation and made no sense.[25]

Imprisoning minors for a "stub that big" presumably made no more sense in 1960 or 1940 than in 1975, but the absurdity was underlined for Senator Hart and others by happening so close to home.

The immediate self-interest of policymakers, however, was embedded in a more personalized typification of marihuana users in general, whether direct kin or not. They were no longer pictured as anonymous, distant others—criminals, Mexican laborers, or even teen-agers; they were someone's sons and daughters. The policy question was no longer simply what to do with "marihuana users" but what to do with "our children." Distant, anonymous "marihuana users" might obviously belong in jail, but "our children" were a different story. As Buckley put the issue in his argument for decriminalization:

Somewhere along the line, the American public decided not to legalize pot. This conclusion, it reached, in my opinion, on the grounds that any different conclusion would appear to capitulate to the counter-culture. . . . *But* at the same time, American parents reached the conclusion, or such is my reading of it, that they did not desire *their* 18-year-old boys and girls to be sent to jail for smoking pot [emphasis added].[26]

Once the perceptions of marihuana users became personalized, assessments of the dangers of the drug were bound to change as well. People who did not want their children or those like them going to jail for marihuana use were particularly receptive to evidence that marihuana was not so dangerous a drug or so great a social problem that it warranted criminal penalties. Had no such evidence been available, of course, many persons might simply have had to live with the cognitive dissonance inherent in opposing harsh penalties for a dangerous drug. In fact, however, throughout the late 1960s and early 1970s, evidence was available to support virtually any position on marihuana. Worried parents, policymakers, and writers, therefore, could seek out reputable experts, books, and testimony that would assure them that marihuana was not that dangerous a drug. "Before we put all our children in jail, let's take an adult look at marihuana," proclaimed the cover of the 1971 paperback edition of Lester Grinspoon's best-selling *Marihuana Reconsidered.* The "adult look" included a demonstration that moderate use of the drug was fairly safe. It thus offered a legitimate resolution to the dilemma of the middle-class parent. Removal of criminal penalties for their children's marihuana use was all right because the drug was not that harmful.[27]

In short, the embourgeoisement of marihuana use effected changes in beliefs about marihuana and in marihuana laws because it generated an image of users as "our children," which was incompatible with an image of marihuana as thoroughly evil and with harsh penalties for use. Prior to the 1960s, when marihuana use was limited to the lower strata, the drug was sometimes pictured as "spreading to youth," but the user never appeared as "someone's child" in discussions of criminal penalties. The typical users appeared simply as criminals from the start or as individuals rapidly turned into criminals by marihuana.

Empathy. The heightened respectability of marihuana users, their increased vociferousness, and their decreased distance from policymakers and writers made their viewpoint more accessible and important. Marihuana users ceased to be merely objects to be controlled; they became subjects who deserved a sympathetic hearing. Prior to the mid-1960s, few persons who set policy or wrote about the drug took time to observe marihuana users in a natural setting, and virtually no one put any credence in what these users said about the drug. Marihuana users simply were not readily accessible nor were they persons whose opinions merited attention, except to debunk.

About 1965, this changed. Reporting on the new "pot problem" on Ivy League campuses, *Time* interviewed collegiate users and recounted with some sympathy their opinion that "pot" was a good drug.[28] Since marihuana users outside of contrived law enforcement settings were likely to laud the marihuana experience and condemn marihuana laws, the new credence given their views inevitably encouraged complementary changes in the attitudes prevalent in public discussion.

Normality. Once policymakers, writers, and middle-class parents in general had the opportunity to observe relatively respectable marihuana users at close range and in everyday contexts, many decided that the users were mostly normal, healthy adolescents except for their drug use. They were not "deviant persons" but merely "normal persons" who happened to commit a few deviant acts. It was a short step from this to conclusions that marihuana use could not have the dreadful effects claimed previously and thus that it did not merit such heavy penalties.

The effects of normalization are evident in a 1970 article by Millicent Hering in *American Libraries*. The author, a "librarian and mother," initially believed that marihuana use was dangerous and that the laws against it were appropriate. She therefore panicked when she realized that her sons and some of her students were occasional users. As she continued to observe them, however, she could not find any obvious signs of other abnormalities:

My two sons were growing into manhood; they brought many young people into our home. My discussions with them continued and I realized that they surely were not killers or psychotics although some of them professed to have smoked the weed. They were, for the most part, lovable, well-adjusted, even scholarly, kids in the process of growing up.[29]

Hering then sought out authoritative information on marihuana. Faced with a welter of conflicting authorities and certain from firsthand experience that marihuana could not be all that terrible, she chose an expert whose opinion corroborated her own observations—Dr. Joel Fort. Fort's work further convinced her that the dangers of marihuana had been exaggerated and that existing laws were unjust. "I'm not for marijuana," she concluded, "but I am against putting young people in jail who do use it."

In short, convinced that their marihuana-using sons and daughters continued to be otherwise normal and confronted with a lack of expert consensus on the dangers of the drug, middle-class parents, legislators, and periodical writers often were predisposed to believe those experts who downplayed the dangers of the drug.

A number of factors were important in this normalization process. It resulted partly from the users' increased respectability. As Troy Duster notes, high-status persons are less easy to stigmatize than low-status persons. It was the product partly of greater accessibility. As Erving Goffman points out, the closer one gets to any social world, the more "meaningful, reasonable, and normal" it appears.[30] Two other factors were clearly important, however. First, marihuana itself, independent of what people believe about it, is simply not a "killer weed." Whatever its total, long-run impact on human beings, it has no spectacular, short-term negative effects on the user. Youthful middle-class users rarely went on violent rampages, became obviously strung out, or fell victim to "overdoses." Had these things happened, the user's respectability and social accessibility might have bred an increased allegiance to stiffer penalties rather than the reverse. Second, there were available experts who were willing to argue that marihuana use was indeed relatively safe. Had such experts not existed, the firsthand experience of normality would have lacked "scientific" corroboration and might have been more readily discounted.

Prior to the mid-1960s, of course, the marihuana user was neither respectable nor socially accessible. Policymakers and the media were unlikely to have firsthand experience with users or to see them as total persons. Thus, there was no basis for the normalization process. Marihuana users were seen purely in the context of deviant behavior and therefore appeared as thoroughly deviant persons.

Political Forces

Kinship, empathy, and normality together constituted a major change in the way in which marihuana use and users were viewed. Anonymous "drug users" became "our children"; objects to be manipulated became subjects to be listened to; and the deviant person became a normal person who happened to engage in certain deviant acts. This shift of framework in turn made public discussion more receptive to positive claims about the effects of marihuana and hence more supportive of marihuana law reform.

Political Actor. The social position of marihuana users not only affected the public typing of them but also gave users themselves some power to shape public discussion of the drug by forcefully voicing their own demands. Youthful middle-class marihuana users became a new collective actor in the drug control arena. Their power was exerted partly in a direct, organized way. Organizations representing both marihuana users (the National Organization for

Reform of Marihuana Laws) and groups with high rates of marihuana use (the National Student Association) sent spokespersons to
congressional hearings on marihuana throughout the period.
Through these official spokespersons, marihuana users made their
support for reduced penalties and their belief in the safety of marihuana use effectively heard. Users also exerted their power in an
indirect, less organized way. In their everyday lives, users vociferously
opposed marihuana laws and claimed their right to smoke. Their
social respectability and their convenient concentration on college
campuses and in high schools made their opposition difficult to
ignore totally. Policymakers and writers became conscious of the
ferment and had to take it into account. Congressional hearings
were suffused with a sense of growing rebellion just beyond the
doors of the hearing chambers. Senator Thomas Dodd, for example,
opened the 1968 Judiciary Committee hearings on juvenile delinquency with the following admonition:

At the same time, we must consider the changing attitudes among our
young people who regard drug use, particularly marihuana use, with alarming
tolerance. We must consider changing public opinion and the surge of
court cases challenging local marihuana laws in various parts of the nation.[31]

He then referred to the "ideological warfare between a segment
of our college youth . . . and police agencies."
        Prior to the mid-1960s, marihuana users—lower in the class
structure and fewer in number—brought no such political pressure
to bear on the policymaking process. There were no organizations
of marihuana users and little formal pressure. The LaGuardia
Report had noted that the average user in New York City in the
1940s "did not indulge in its use with a spirit of braggadocio or
as a challenge to law," and Richard Blum has pointed out the
quiescence of even the beatnik user of the 1950s.[32]
        Political Audience. Perhaps more important than being a political
actor, marihuana users after the mid-1960s provided a visible,
respectable, appreciative audience for those public health officials,
intellectuals, scientists, and physicians who were interested in debunking the established beliefs and policy regarding marihuana.
As noted in the previous chapter, opposition to the Narcotics Bureau's
view of marihuana had existed since the late 1940s, but it had been

muted, and dissidents had never launched a frontal assault on the established marihuana consensus.

By the late 1960s, this had changed dramatically. Congressional hearings and the media were full of criticisms of existing beliefs and policy by "reputable experts," public health officials, professional and scientific organizations, and individual physicians and social scientists.[33] To an extent, the upsurge of reputable expert criticism simply reflected the growing strength of a health establishment and its increased efforts to shape drug control policy in general.

This was only part of the story, however. Another cause of the health establishment's newly found activism concerning marihuana was that for the first time in the United States there existed a large, educated, vociferous constituency that was receptive to expert research, writing, and testimony that challenged the harmfulness of marihuana and the propriety of harsh penalties. Prior to the mid-1960s, dissident officials and intellectuals had no natural audience to address; now they did.

A symbiotic relationship, then, developed between marihuana users and a mixed bag of health officials, physicians, scientists, and intellectuals. Without identifying with the drug culture, the experts gave precise formulation and legitimacy to the beliefs and demands of the users; without regarding the health establishment as their official representatives, the users provided the experts with an interested audience to address.[34]

Arguments About the Law

In various ways the changes just described increased the interest in and sensitivity to "positive" (exculpatory) information on marihuana. The inevitable conclusion was a reassessment of the drug. Marihuana was deemed by many to be significantly less dangerous than had been previously believed. This judgment in turn became an important argument in favor of reducing penalties for use. Marihuana use was simply not dangerous enough to warrant long prison sentences.

The danger argument, however, was not the only or even the primary argument in favor of reduced penalties. It was not accepted by all proponents of reform and did not figure prominently at many points in the marihuana debates of the late 1960s and early 1970s. The most common arguments made in favor of reducing or removing criminal penalties for use were what we shall call the *criminality, credibility,* and *career* arguments, each of which reflected the middle-class position of the marihuana users.

Criminality. The criminality argument asserted that harsh penalties for marihuana use were inappropriate because the users were not really "criminals," except for their actual drug use. The designation of users as noncriminals was meant in both a narrow and a broad sense. Narrowly conceived, it meant simply that unlike the users of other drugs, marihuana users generally did not commit any major street crimes, such as burglary, robbery, or homicide. Broadly conceived, it meant that the users came from a "respectable" social background and simply did not belong in prison. The case for the noncriminality of the user thus rested as much on the user's social and educational position as on his lack of criminal record. Psychiatrist Helen Nowlis, for example, argued against criminal penalties for marihuana and LSD users in the following terms:

I feel very stongly that unless one defines criminal in terms of the way in which you set up the law, in terms of the concept criminal, that the overwhelming majority of them are not.[35]

To support her contention, Nowlis cited the case of a young man convicted of a felony for selling three LSD sugar cubes. She noted that the offender was a college graduate with a good grade point average and a long list of reputable extracurricular activities. "Is this a criminal in the ordinary sense of criminality?" she pleaded.

Similar arguments were made by a group of college-based psychiatrists and by the American Orthopsychiatric Association:

Therefore we advise against criminal penalties and legislation directed at marijuana use which, if strictly enforced at present, could lead to branding as criminal a portion of American youth to whom we look for constructive social contribution and leadership.[36]

The Association has substantial doubt whether the mere possession of marihuana is a proper basis for the imposition of any federal penalties, let alone the lengthy prison terms which the Administration's bill would impose. This conclusion is rooted in considerations which go substantially beyond the relative lack of dangerousness in marihuana use. Among the foremost considerations should be the fact that untold millions of fine

young Americans use marihuana at least on an occasion. These are youths
who have no criminal tendencies whatsoever and who often exemplify
admirable character traits.[37]

In each case there was an exquisite sensitivity to the users' social
status and what they did beyond the narrow context of the criminal
law. The tacit assumption was that the character of the user, as
well as the nature of use itself, ought to be taken into account in
making the law.

   Credibility. A second argument against harsh penalties was that
they were not credible with marihuana users and therefore were
ineffective deterrents. Users, it was argued, strongly believed that
marihuana was less dangerous than many legal drugs and that they
had a right to use it. They thus had no respect for marihuana laws
and were in open conflict with law enforcement authorities. In
such circumstances, marihuana laws could hardly have a deterrent
effect. Reestablishing the effectiveness of these laws and the credibility of those who enforced them would require at least a partial
reduction in penalties.

   Career. A final rationale for reducing penalties was that a felony
conviction or a prison sentence might ruin the career of the offender.
Writing in the *National Review,* Richard Cowan urged conservatives
to rethink their support for criminal penalties by pointing to "lives
disrupted and even ruined, families divided, records besmirched,
a life of ostracism."[38] Despite its opposition to outright legaliza-
tion, in 1968 the American Medical Association's Council on Mental
Health objected to heavy penalties for

the youthful experimenter who, by incurring a criminal record through a
single thoughtless act, places his future career in jeopardy. The lives of
many young people are being needlessly damaged.[39]

The core of the career argument, however it was expressed, was a
preoccupation with the potential damage that criminal penalties
could do to the future lives of those young people convicted for use.[40]

   What is striking about all three of these arguments—criminality,
credibility, career—is that they originated in the late 1960s. Prior
to that time, no one thought to question whether or not the marihuana
user was really a criminal; no one worried about the credibility of

the law among users; and no one pondered the possible effects of conviction and imprisonment on the user's future life. Marihuana users were simply presumed to be "criminals" in every sense of the term, and no distinction was drawn between the character of the user and the nature of the act. Users were neither powerful nor respectable enough for their opinions about the law to matter and hence for credibility to be an issue. Finally, they were not seen as persons with futures or careers that could be ruined. These issues were not explicitly discussed because they were not problematic as long as users were drawn primarily from the lower strata and marginal groups.[41]

With the increase in youthful middle-class users in the 1960s, this changed. Because of their social background, these new users were unlikely to appear to be involved in major street crime. Furthermore, they were likely to be respectable in other ways and thus did not possess the auxiliary traits of the criminal status. It therefore became difficult to regard them as criminal persons simply because they had committed the criminal act of marihuana use. Similarly, the new users had the power and status to command attention, so their attitude toward the law had to be taken into account in shaping policy. Finally, middle-class youth generally were presumed to be going somewhere: They had futures; they were building careers. Therefore, the issue of how a marihuana conviction would affect those futures became relevant.

In short, the rise of youthful middle-class marihuana use changed the terms in which marihuana laws were discussed and broadened the range of arguments that could be made legitimately against existing marihuana laws. This buttressed the case for law reform and made support for such reforms more likely.

CONCLUSION

The new middle-class position of the late 1960s, early 1970s marihuana user affected marihuana laws by altering the dominant stereotypes of the user, by adding new political forces to the drug control arena, and by generating new arguments against existing laws. None of these effects probably was decisive in itself; rather, each contributed to the other and to the ultimate outcome.

Perhaps the crucial factor was the change in ideology, in the system of beliefs that framed public discussion of the drug. The increase in marihuana use by middle-class youth directly and dramatically altered the ideological framework within which the drug and laws concerning it were publicly discussed. These pervasive changes in the terms of public discussion favored a reassessment of the drug's dangers and the reform of marihuana laws.

The transformation of the ideological framework was neither explicit nor recognized by everyone involved. What changed was the tacit understanding of how the marihuana issue should be discussed. It now seemed natural to typify marihuana users as "someone's children" rather than as anonymous others. Whereas once such a question was unthinkable, it now seemed appropriate to question how a conviction for marihuana use would affect the user's future career. Because these new ways of discussing the marihuana issue seemed so obviously "right," hardly anyone realized how novel they were.

These changes in the taken-for-granted put new constraints on public discussion and thus reshaped the terrain on which individual and social actors fought out the marihuana issue. It is, therefore, misleading to see marihuana law reform as resulting simply from the conscious, organized efforts of self-interested policymakers and politically mobilized marihuana users. The reassessment of marihuana's dangers and the support for law reform of some kind were simply too broad and too pervasive to be explained by these factors alone. Self-interested policymakers and politically mobilized marihuana users operated in a changed ideological framework that was receptive to their view of marihuana and their arguments for law reform.

NOTES

1. U.S., Senate, Committee on the Judiciary, *Narcotic Rehabilitation Act of 1966*, 89th Cong., 2d sess., 1966, pp. 175-176, 385, 449, 458-460.

2. Stanley Einstein, ed., *Proceedings of the First International Conference on Student Drug Surveys* (Farmingdale, N.Y.: Baywood, 1972), p. 199.

3. Allen Ginsberg, "The Great Marihuana Hoax," *The Atlantic Monthly*, November 1966, pp. 104, 107-112.

4. U.S., Senate, Committee on the Judiciary, Subcommittee to Investigate the Administration of the Internal Security Act and Other Internal Security Laws, *Marihuana-Hashish Epidemic and Its Impact on United States Security*, 94th Cong., 1st sess., 1975, p. v.

5. "Pot Problem," *Time*, 12 March 1965, p. 49.

6. Joel Fort, "Drug Use and the Law: A Case for Legalizing Marijuana," *Current*, December 1969, pp. 4-13.

7. These descriptions are found, for example, in "Marihuana: Millions of Turned-on Users," *Life*, 7 July 1967, pp. 16-23; "Mild Intoxicant," *Scientific American*, February 1969, pp. 42-43; Lester Grinspoon, "Marihuana," *Scientific American*, December 1969, pp. 17-25; Millicent B. Hering, "The Law and Maryjane," *American Libraries*, October 1970, pp. 896-899.

8. Antoni Gollan, "The Great Marihuana Problem," *National Review*, 30 January 1968, pp. 74-80.

9. "To Parents: Plain Talk on Marijuana," *Business Week*, 21 March 1970, p. 121; "The Latest Medical Facts About Marihuana," *Good Housekeeping*, May 1971, pp. 185-186.

10. Benjamin Spock, "Preventing Drug Abuse in Children," *Redbook*, May 1971, p. 36.

11. U.S., President's Commission on Law Enforcement and the Administration of Justice, *Task Force: Narcotics and Drug Abuse* (Washington, D.C.: U.S. Government Printing Office, 1967), pp. 12-14, 24-26, 126-131.

12. U.S., National Commission on Marihuana and Drug Abuse, *Marihuana: A Signal of Misunderstanding* (Washington, D.C.: U.S. Government Printing Office, 1972), pp. 90-91.

13. These hearings included the following: U.S., Senate, Committee on the Judiciary, *Narcotic Legislation*, 91st Cong., 1st sess., 1969; U.S., Senate, Committee on Labor and Public Welfare, Special Subcommittee on Alcoholism and Narcotics, *Federal Drug Abuse and Drug Dependence Prevention, Treatment, and Rehabilitation Act of 1970*, 91st Cong., 2d sess., 1970; U.S., House of Representatives, Committee on Ways and Means, *Controlled Dangerous Substances, Narcotics, and Drug Control Laws*, 91st Cong., 2d sess., 1970; U.S., House of Representatives, Committee on Interstate and Foreign Commerce, *Drug Abuse Control Amendments—1970*, 91st Cong., 2d sess., 1970.

14. Federal Bureau of Narcotics, "The Dangers of Marihuana—Facts You Should Know," in *Marihuana*, ed. Stanley E. Grupp (Columbus, Ohio: Charles E. Merrill, 1971), pp. 78-84; Donald E. Miller, "Legislative and Judicial Trends in Marihuana Control," in *Marihuana*, ed. Grupp, pp. 297-302; Donald E. Miller, "Marijuana and Legal Controls," in *Marijuana*, ed. Erich Goode (New York: Atherton, 1970), pp. 155-171.

15. This view of alcohol is itself of relatively recent vintage. The nineteenth-century temperance view held that safe, moderate drinking was impossible. See Harry Levine, "Demon of the Middle Class: Self-control, Liquor, and the Ideology of Temperance in 19th-century America" (Ph.D. diss., University of California, Berkeley, 1978).

16. For summaries of how marihuana laws changed in the 1960s and

1970s, see Richard J. Bonnie and Charles Whitebread II, "History of Marihuana Legislation," in *Marihuana: A Signal of Misunderstanding*, ed. National Commission on Marihuana and Drug Abuse, Appendix I, pp. 491-498; Harvey R. Levine, *Legal Dimensions of Drug Abuse in the United States* (Springfield, Ill.: Charles Thomas, 1974); Michael P. Rosenthal, "The Legislative Response to Marihuana: When the Shoe Pinches Enough," *Journal of Drug Issues* 7 (1977):61-77; Richard C. Schroeder, *The Politics of Drugs*, 2d rev. ed. (Washington, D.C.: Congressional Quarterly, 1980).

17. U.S., House of Representatives, Committee on Interstate and Foreign Commerce, *Increased Control Over Hallucinogens and Other Dangerous Drugs*, 90th Cong., 2d sess., 1968, pp. 101-103; House of Representatives, *Controlled Dangerous Substances*, pp. 193-211.

18. Rosenthal, "Legislative Response."

19. National Commission, *Marihuana*, pp. 127-167.

20. Schroeder, *Politics of Drugs*.

21. National Organization for the Reform of Marihuana Laws, "The Marijuana Issue" (1977), p. 12.

22. Gollan, "Great Marihuana Problem"; Richard Cowan, "American Conservatives Should Revise Their Position on Marihuana," *National Review*, 8 December 1972, pp. 1344-1346; Buckley, "End the Pot Penalties," *Washington Star-News*, 10 November 1974; Kilpatrick, "Thoughts on Marihuana," *Washington Star-News*, 4 December 1974.

23. Senate, *Marihuana-Hashish Epidemic*, p. 125. See also Senator Eastland's introduction and Robert Kolodny's testimony, pp. v-xx, 117-126.

24. William F. Buckley, Jr., "Private Enterprise and Dope," *National Review*, 8 September 1970, p. 964.

25. U.S., Senate, Committee on the Judiciary, *Marijuana Decriminalization*, 94th Cong., 1st sess., 1975, p. 6.

26. Buckley, "End the Pot Penalties."

27. Lester Grinspoon, *Marihuana Reconsidered* (New York: Bantam, 1971).

28. "Pot Problem," *Time*.

29. Hering, "The Law and Maryjane."

30. Troy Duster, *The Legislation of Morality* (New York: Free Press, 1970); Erving Goffman, *Asylums* (Garden City, N.Y.: Doubleday, 1961), p. x.

31. U.S., Senate, Committee on the Judiciary, Subcommittee to Investigate Juvenile Delinquency, *Juvenile Delinquency*, 90th Cong., 2d sess., 1968, pp. 4328-4329.

32. David Solomon, ed., *The Marihuana Papers* (New York: New American Library, 1966), p. 295; Richard H. Blum and Associates, *Utopiates* (New York: Atherton Press, 1964), p. 3.

33. The term "reputable expert" denotes those persons who by virtue

of educational credentials and official position can legitimately claim expertise on matters of drug use and drug control. It does not presume a judgment on the quality or validity of their ideas.

34. For the importance of the audience in shaping the artistic and intellectual message, see Kenneth Burke, *The Philosophy of Literary Form* (New York: Vintage, 1957), pp. 191-200.

35. Senate, *Juvenile Delinquency*, 1968, p. 4505-4506.

36. House of Representatives, *Hallucinogens,* p. 229.

37. Senate, *Narcotics Legislation,* p. 934.

38. Cowan, "American Conservatives."

39. Council on Mental Health, "Marihuana and Society," in *Marihuana,* ed. Grupp, p. 56.

40. For additional examples of criminality, credibility, and career arguments, see the following: Senate, *Narcotics Legislation,* pp. 245-246, 301-302, 663-683; Senate, *Federal Drug Abuse Prevention,* p. 194; House of Representatives, *Controlled Dangerous Substances,* pp. 199-204, 331-344, 449ff.; House of Representatives, *Drug Abuse Control Amendments,* pp. 549-556, 568-575; Senate, *Marijuana Decriminalization,* pp. 2, 49-96.

41. As noted in chapter 4, although marihuana was seen in the 1930s primarily as a drug "spreading to youth," it never became a drug "of youth." Thus stereotypes of use and user were never adjusted accordingly.

FROM KILLER WEED   7
TO DROP-OUT DRUG

Among those who persisted in seeing marihuana as a dangerous drug, the characterization of that danger changed dramatically in the mid-1960s. What had once been regarded as a "killer weed" became seen as a "drop-out drug." This change can get lost easily amid the loud debates over the legality and morality of marihuana use, but it is nonetheless significant. It involved a shift not only in the specific dangers claimed for marihuana use but also, and more importantly, in the general image of the drug and its users. It entailed nothing less than a transformation of the assumptions framing the public discussion of marihuana.

We have traced the emergence of the image of marihuana as a drug that made its users violent, criminal, and aggressive. Perhaps the clearest statement of this pre-1960s "killer weed" image was made by antidrug crusaders Earle and Robert Rowell in 1939: "While opium Kills ambition and Deadens initiative, marihuana incites to immorality and crime."[1]

In the turbulent debate over marihuana beginning in the 1960s, this image was widely replaced by the opposite assertion that marihuana induced passivity and destroyed motivation. What the Rowells had once said about opium in contrast to marihuana now was said about marihuana itself: It killed ambition and deadened initiative; it created an amotivational syndrome; it was a "drop-out drug."

Thus, in summarizing the drug's effects, *Time* argued in 1965 that marihuana "affects user's judgment and if used daily will dull a student's initiative"; and Benjamin Spock, the pediatrician and political activist, noted in 1971 that "a small percentage of users, the 'potheads', make its frequent use the focus of their existence and lose some of their ambition and aim."[2]

We shall document the rise of the "drop-out drug" image and explain its emergence in terms of three social conditions: the declining influence of narcotics officials on public discussion, the proliferation of marihuana use among middle-class youth, and the new role of marihuana as a symbol of the Counterculture. These three conditions correspond respectively to the three guiding concepts presented in chapter 1: entrepreneurship, social locus, and symbolic politics. The symbolic meaning of marihuana was especially important in shaping the image of the drug, and we shall accordingly dwell upon it.

A discussion of the "drop-out drug" image inevitably leads to a consideration of what we have called the "Hippie Hypothesis." This argues that in the late 1960s, marihuana became a symbol of intergenerational conflict and thus of hedonism, radicalism, permissiveness, rejection of authority, and other features of the period's youthful Counterculture. Objections to the drug became based on what it represented, not on its effects. Opposing marihuana use and supporting antimarihuana laws became a symbolic way of condemning the Counterculture and asserting the validity of the dominant culture.

The "Hippie Hypothesis" is partly right. It is undoubtedly correct to see marihuana as a symbol in the wider cultural and political conflict of the day, but it is misleading to argue that marihuana was rejected for what it represented, not because of its effects. To draw so sharp a distinction between the drug's meaning and its perceived effects does not do justice to the complexity of the public discussion of marihuana at the time. The two were inextricably mixed together, for what the drug symbolized helped to shape the effects imputed to it. We can understand the dynamics of symbolism at work here by examining the "drop-out drug" image and its causal roots.

RISE OF THE DROP-OUT DRUG

The once common belief that marihuana made the user aggressive and violent virtually disappeared in the late 1960s. The Federal

Bureau of Narcotics and its various organizational successors *did* attempt to purvey the violence image, but few accepted it. During the 1966 Senate Judiciary Committee hearings on the Narcotic Rehabilitation Act, FBN Commissioner Henry Giordano, who had succeeded Harry Anslinger in 1962, offered the following time-honored assessment of the dangers of marihuana use:

From my studies and experience, one theme emerges—that marihuana is capable of inducing acts of violence, even murder. The drug frees the unconscious tendencies of the individual user, the result being reflected in frequent quarrels, fights, and assaults.[3]

To support this contention, Giordano offered the standard FBN data—examples of marihuana-induced individual violence in the United States and collective violence in non-Western countries.

Giordano repeated his claim at the 1968 House hearings on control of LSD, but this was the last time that any major witness mentioned the connection between marihuana and violence.[4] Testimony at Senate hearings on juvenile delinquency and drug use in the same year and on narcotic addiction and drug abuse in 1969 linked marihuana use to automobile accidents, acute psychotic reactions, and the amotivational syndrome but not to violence.[5] The violence claim was absent also from the series of hearings in 1969 and 1970 on the Comprehensive Drug Abuse Prevention and Control Act and was ignored even by the 1974 hearings on the "marihuana-hashish epidemic," which made a concerted effort to publicize every possible marihuana-related danger. The National Commission on Marihuana and Drug Abuse concluded that "marihuana does not cause violent or aggressive behavor."[6]

The bureau's view of marihuana, in short, no longer dominated public discussion as it once had. Quite the contrary; narcotics officials now seemed to be pushed along in a wider flow. By 1971, John Ingersoll, head of the Bureau of Narcotics and Dangerous Drugs, had largely given up the violence claim and was describing marihuana as "psychologically habituating, often resulting in an amotivational syndrome."[7]

The violence claim disappeared from the media as well. In the *Readers' Guide* sample from the 1964-1976 period, only one (2 percent) of the forty-three articles that discussed the effects of marihuana mentioned violence, compared to 57 percent in the pre-1964 period and

85 percent in the late 1930s (see Table 10). At the same time, numerous articles explicitly denied that marihuana made the user violent.

Table 10
VIOLENCE

Time Period	Articles Mentioning	Articles Not Mentioning	Relevant N^a
1964-1976	1 (2%)	42 (98%)	43 (100%)
1935-1940	17 (85%)	3 (15%)	20 (100%)
1890-1963	24 (57%)	18 (43%)	42 (100%)

1935-1940 vs. 1964-1976   Corrected Chi Square^b= 41.8 p<.001
1890-1963 vs. 1964-1976   Corrected Chi Square = 28.1 p<.001

[a]Relevant N refers to the total number of articles mentioning at least one effect.
[b]All chi squares calculated using Yates's correction.

The Stepping-stone Hypothesis, which formed the basis of the case against marihuana in the 1950s, fared only somewhat better. To be sure, progression to "harder" drugs was mentioned as a danger of marihuana use by 16 percent of the articles, and the National Commission on Marihuana and Drug Abuse heard testimony in 1971 that lax enforcement of marihuana laws inevitably would engender a heroin epidemic in the near future.[8] This claim, however, was losing popularity too. The Stepping-stone Hypothesis was denied more often than it was affirmed and was rarely the focus of attention.

As the violence and stepping-stone claims declined in importance, other alleged dangers of marihuana became prominent. Marihuana intoxication was said to cause "acute psychotic reactions" (roughly equivalent to the "temporary insanity" of the pre-1964 period but without any hint of violence) and to impair driving ability by interfering with psychomotor functioning. The time-honored belief that chronic marihuana use caused wholesale mental and physical deterioration was recast with the help of a wealth of new research into a number of more specific claims. Witnesses at Senator Eastland's 1974 hearings on the "marihuana-hashish epidemic" argued that chronic use caused brain damage, lung disease, fetal deaths and abnormalities, chromosome damage, lowered testosterone levels, and impaired immune response.[9] Finally, it was routinely asserted that although marihuana definitely was not physically addicting, it did lead to a psychological habituation (or emotional dependence) in which the user became totally involved in drug use (see Table 11).

Table 11
EFFECTS, 1964-1976

(Total N = 59)

Effect	Articles Mentioning[a]
Violence	1 (2%)
Passivity	15 (35%)
Addiction	0
Dependence	9 (21%)
Stepping-stone	7 (16%)
Accidents	8 (19%)
Debauchery	0
Unpredictability	1 (2%)
Miscellaneous acute effects	14 (33%)
Miscellaneous long-term effects	9 (21%)
Relevant N[b]	43 (100%)

[a]Percentages do not total 100 because several articles mention more than one effect.
[b]Relevant N refers to the total number of articles mentioning at least one effect.

The danger most commonly attributed to marihuana in the 1964-1976 period, however, was the "amotivational syndrome." Long-term marihuana use was said to destroy ambition and initiative, to interfere with the effort to cope with the world, and to facilitate withdrawal from reality. It led, in the words of the commission, to "lethargy, instability, social deterioration, a loss of interest in virtually all activities other than drug use."[10]

Like the violence claim of an earlier day, the amotivational syndrome claim implied that marihuana use destroyed the user's self-control and released the basically antisocial human nature previously held in check. The difference lay in how this underlying human nature was pictured. According to the violence claim, marihuana released a fundamentally destructive, aggressive human nature and thus caused a failure of restraint. According to the amotivational syndrome claim, marihuana uncovered an essentially passive, ambitionless human nature and thus produced a failure of achievement. In short, the central characterization of the adverse effects of marihuana use shifted in the mid-1960s from a failure of restraint to a failure of achievement.

It is tempting to see in the shift from violence to amotivational syndrome a change from a "public safety" perspective to a "public health" perspective. This is accurate to an extent. According to the violence claim, users were primarily threats to others and hence constituted a law enforcement problem. In contrast, according to the amotivational syndrome, they were primarily threats to themselves and hence represented a health problem. The public safety/public health distinction, however, also implies a shift in characterization of the user from sinner to victim that did not occur. Whether considered a violent criminal or a drop-out, the marihuana user was viewed ambivalently as partially culpable for his condition and partially a victim of the wiles of the drug.

The amotivational syndrome appeared in 35 percent of the periodical articles from 1964 to 1976, substantially more than the 12 percent figure for the pre-1964 period and the 15 percent figure for the late 1930s. Although found in less than a majority of articles, it was still the most cited adverse effect of marihuana. No one claim dominated the periodical discussion of marihuana in the 1964-1976 period as violence had in the 1930s, because no one organization monopolized the social definition of reality as the Federal Bureau of Narcotics had in that previous era (see Table 12).[11]

Despite the plurality of authorities and opinions, however, the amotivational syndrome did dominate judicial deliberations, congressional hearings, and federal reports on marihuana. In his landmark 1967 decision upholding the constitutionality of Massachusetts's marihuana law, Judge G. Joseph Tauro described marihuana use as follows:

Many succumb to the drug as a handy means of withdrawing from the inevitable stresses and legitimate demands of society. The evasion of problems and escape from reality seem to be among the desired effects of the use of marijuana.[12]

Table 12
PASSIVITY

Time Period	Articles Mentioning	Articles Not Mentioning	Relevant N^a
1964-1976	15 (35%)	28 (65%)	43 (100%)
1935-1940	3 (15%)	17 (85%)	20 (100%)
1890-1963	5 (12%)	37 (88%)	42 (100%)

1935-1940 *vs.* 1964-1976   Corrected Chi Square^b= 2.2 p<.20
1890-1963 *vs.* 1964-1976   Corrected Chi Square = 5.3 p<.05

[a]Relevant N refers to the total number of articles mentioning at least one effect.
[b]All chi squares calculated using Yates's correction.

The charge of passivity and withdrawal was first voiced in congressional hearings in 1968 by Dr. Donald Louria of the New York State Council on Drug Addiction:

Drug-induced withdrawal is a problem of increasing severity in our society, and LSD is only one vehicle for this. Even marihuana in heavy doses can, after repeated use, produce the same loss of ambition, rejection of previously established goals, and retreat into a solipsistic, drug-oriented cocoon.[13]

In the 1969-1970 hearings on drug control reorganization, the amotivational syndrome was the major claim made against marihuana; it was mentioned in eight of the eleven pieces of testimony that discussed adverse effects.[14] It was, moreover, the only danger that was stressed or discussed at length. For example, Roger Egeberg, assistant secretary for health and scientific affairs in HEW, made the following point:

Marihuana use particularly because it starts at such an early age is apt to make many people go off into a pleasant euphoria or other means of evading reality at a time, 15, 16, 17, 18 years when they should be setting their aims. . . . *This I would say is the tragedy to all of society with respect to the use of marihuana* [emphasis added].[15]

Dana Fornsworth of the Harvard University Health Services also focused on the amotivational syndrome.

But I am very much concerned about what has come to be called the "amotivational syndrome" [emphasis added]. I am certain as I can be . . . that when an individual becomes dependent upon marihuana . . . he becomes preoccupied with it. His attitude changes toward endorsement of values which he had not before; he tends to become very easily satisfied with what is immediately present, in such a way that he seems to have been robbed of his ability to make appropriate choices.[16]

The 1972 report of the National Commission on Marihuana and Drug Abuse took the amotivational syndrome more seriously than any other potential adverse effect of marihuana. It denied that marihuana use led to acute psychotic reactions except in "rare cases" or among a "predisposed few" and doubted that "significant physical, biochemical, or mental abnormalities could be attributed solely to . . . marihuana smoking." It concluded that the "weight of evidence is that marihuana does not cause violent or aggressive behavior" and that "recent research has not yet proven that marihuana use significantly impairs driving ability or performance." It also found no evidence of addiction, progression to harder drugs, or chromosome damage and birth defects. In contrast, the report was careful to stress that the amotivational syndrome was the real danger for heavy users and might become a major problem in the United States as use increased.[17]

More importantly, the commission was sensitive to the fact that Americans were particularly worried about the amotivational syndrome. In discussing "why society feels threatened," the report noted that parents were concerned that "marihuana will undermine or interfere with academic and vocational career development and achievement" or even worse, that it will lead to "amotivation" and "dropping out."[18] The commission itself denied that marihuana as then used was an important causal factor in either "dropping down" or "dropping out," but the very fact that it took time to do so indicates the social importance of these claims.

Senator Eastland's 1974 hearings pictured the amotivational syndrome as the most significant behavioral effect of marihuana use.

The most notable and consistent clinical changes that have been reported in heavy marihuana smokers include apathy approaching indolence, lack of motivation . . . reduced interest in socializing, and attraction to intense sensory stimuli.

Possibly the issue of greatest importance in the area of behavioral toxicity of marihuana is the question of the amotivational syndrome.[19]

The amotivational syndrome was mentioned by twelve of the fourteen witnesses who testified on the behavioral effects of marihuana—several times as often as any other adverse effect—and it was the only behavioral effect to be systematically discussed.[20]

Beyond its mere quantitative predominance, the amotivational syndrome also provided a basis for understanding the other adverse effects of marihuana and for constructing an image of the user as a person. It thus played the same pivotal cognitive role that violence did in the 1930s. Psychological dependence, the second most frequently mentioned adverse effect in the late 1960s and early 1970s, was basically a synonym for the amotivational syndrome: Both claims implied that the heavy marihuana user became totally wrapped up in drug use and lost interest in everything else. The lowered testosterone levels in males and brain damage caused by marihuana use were partly interpreted as the direct causes of the amotivational syndrome. The latter was said to limit the user's cognitive ability to deal with the world and the former to lead to a general reduction in drive.[21] The putative link between marihuana use and automobile accidents was understood to result from the user's reduced desire and ability to cope with the world.

Those who sought to typify users implicitly described them as embodiments of the amotivational syndrome. Passivity, lack of motivation, withdrawal from reality, and an inability to cope were seen not as some of the user's many traits, but as master traits that defined his very being. In Judge Tauro's adjectival overkill, marihuana users were "the disaffiliated, the neurotic and psychotic, the confused, the anxious, the alienated, the inadequate, the weak."[22] For University of California, Berkeley, medical physicist Hardin Jones, the amotivational syndrome was nothing less than a whole lifestyle of "dropping out, indolence, lowering of goals, alienation," and "kookiness."[23]

In short, the amotivational syndrome was not simply one important effect imputed to marihuana. It formed the core of the dominant image of both drug and user. Marihuana did not simply cause an amotivatonal syndrome among other things; it was in essence a "drop-out drug."

MARIHUANA AND THE COUNTERCULTURE

The rise of the "drop-out drug" image can be seen as the result of the demise of the dominance of narcotics officials over public discussion, the increase in middle-class marihuana use, and most importantly, the emergence of marihuana as a symbol of the Counterculture.

In the early 1960s, President Kennedy initiated a series of White House conferences, panels, and commissions on "narcotics and drug abuse" that effectively opened up the discussion of marihuana to other government agencies and interested groups.[24] Later in the decade, the rapid increase in marihuana use made the drug a major social issue for the first time. It became the subject of widespread popular debate, headlines, and endless hearings and reports. The basis of the dominance of the marihuana issue by narcotics officials was thus undermined. Marihuana became an important matter; other interested groups (notably scientists, physicians, and public health officials) became involved; users themselves became a force in their own right; and the general populace was aroused. What once had been a small-scale, uninterrupted monologue became a wide-ranging, raucous cacophony of voices, and narcotics officials could not hope to dominate a public discussion of such scale and diversity. The main proponent of the "killer weed" image thus lost ground, while the diversity of voices created the opportunity for a new image of marihuana to emerge.

The emergence of this new image was brought about partly by the rise of youthful middle-class marihuana users. In the 1920s and 1930s, when Mexican laborers and other lower-strata groups had been perceived as the primary users of marihuana, the drug had been seen as creating the kind of deviant behavior regarded as typical of those groups—aggression or a failure of restraint. As marihuana use among middle-class youth increased rapidly in the 1960s, the image of the drug shifted accordingly. If violence was the kind of deviance expected from lower-strata groups, then a failure to achieve, a loss of motivation and initiative, appeared to be the typical way that middle-class kids went bad and the ultimate failure of middle-class socialization. They were expected not to commit violent crimes or go insane in any spectacular way but rather to drop out or squander their potential. The dangers attributed to marihuana changed from the deviance expected from the older using group to that expected from the newer group. The "killer weed" became a "drop-out drug."

Above all, the image of marihuana changed because the drug became a symbol in the wider struggle between the dominant society and the Counterculture. As used here, "Counterculture" refers to the political and cultural rebellion of middle-class youth during the late 1960s and early 1970s, as well as to those who participated in this rebellion in its widest sense—not only those who became involved in radical politics or experimented with alternative life-styles but also the much larger number who shared the sense of alienation and the value commitments that fostered these activities.

"Symbol" has two quite different meanings. In one sense, a symbol is something that refers conceptually to something else. Thus rain is a symbol for precipitation of a certain kind, horse a symbol for a particular species of four-legged animal, and Counter-culture a symbol of the youthful rebellion of the late 1960s, early 1970s. In each case, the word is a conceptual designation of the object. In a second sense, a symbol is something that not only refers to but also embodies something else and thus is responded to as if it were that other thing. It evokes in us the same experience as the object it symbolizes. This usage is nicely described by Gertrude Jaeger and Philip Selznick:

The symbol itself takes on the human significance possessed by its referent. To the naturalist, the flock of birds may be a sign of land, and nothing more. To the sailor long at sea, the flock of birds may acquire symbolic status and he may respond to them much as he will later respond to his actual homecoming. Black may be merely a denotative sign of death, death merely a natural sign of disease. But when black is a true symbol of death, we respond to it much as we would humanly respond in the presence of death.[25]

We are concerned here about marihuana as a symbol in this second sense. For many persons in the late 1960s and early 1970s, marihuana not only was associated with the Counterculture but also came to embody it: They responded to the one as if it were the other.

The symbolic status of marihuana was sometimes directly acknowledged in public discussion, and an effort was occasionally made to distinguish the drug's *effects* from its *meaning*. As a 1971 *National Review* article put it, "That appears to me to be the nub of the pot problem: The weed is an adjunct, forcing tool and instrument of initiation for a lifestyle that generally rejects or seeks to bring down 'ordered life as we know it.'"[26] The following year in the same journal, Jeffrey Hart was even more explicit, arguing that the evils of marihuana lay in its meaning, not its effects ("I care not a fig for its physical effects"): Marihuana symbolized the Counterculture, and the main purpose of antimarihuana laws was "to lean on, to penalize the Counterculture."[27]

For their part, proponents of penalty reduction often took pains to argue that marihuana should not be regarded as anything more than a drug. The national commission explicitly "tried to desymbolize" marihuana so as to build support for decriminalization.[28]

Public discussion of marihuana, however, rarely drew such a neat distinction between meaning and effects, and the most significant consequence of the transformation of marihuana into a symbol lay in the way the effects themselves were reconceptualized. The relationship of marihuana to the Counterculture was not in itself a major issue in the discussion of the drug's dangers or in the debate over penalty reduction. Contrary to the Hippie Hypothesis, the objection to marihuana and to marihuana law reform was based primarily on the harmful physical and psychological effects of the drug as policymakers and the media perceived them, not on the lifestyle associated with it. Opposition to the drug was conceptualized in terms of what it did, not in terms of the culture it symbolized or was tied to. The relationship between marihuana and the Counterculture was rarely raised in congressional hearings or periodical articles. When it was mentioned, it was usually a matter of fact, not as a major reason to oppose the drug.

In short, the symbolic status of marihuana did not render its effects as a drug unimportant in public discussion; rather it shaped how these effects were discussed. Here lies the truly important consequence of the transformation of marihuana into a symbol. When the harmful effects of the drug upon the individual were discussed, they were described in a way determined by the fact that marihuana was the symbolic embodiment of the Counterculture. The social characteristics of the Counterculture, as perceived by the dominant society, were projected onto marihuana and then said to be psychological effects inherent in the drug. Because the Counterculture was characterized as passive and escapist, marihuana became seen as a producer of passivity and escape on the individual level. The amotivational syndrome, in other words, was simply the Counterculture writ small and turned into a psychiatric diagnosis.

Once established, this new image of marihuana persisted because it was functional: It reinforced a way of explaining the Counterculture that was simultaneously a way of explaining it away, of accounting for it without having to come to terms with it. The easiest way to condemn youthful rebellion was to describe it in purely negative terms—as dropping out from organized social life, as escaping from reality, as failure. In this way, the adult generation and the dominant society did not have to acknowledge and deal with what youth were doing, but only with what youth were *not* doing. They did not have to confront the youthful rebels' philosophical, moral, and political commitments or the alternative world that they were trying to build in however halting, half-hearted, and incomplete a way.

The image of marihuana as a source of an amotivational syndrome facilitated this purely negative view of the Counterculture, because if the amotivational syndrome was simply the Counterculture writ small, the Counterculture could be seen simply as the amotivational syndrome writ large. The amotivational syndrome provided a seemingly simple, delimited model on the psychological level for understanding a more complex, diffuse, and thus harder-to-grasp phenomenon on the cultural level.

Contemplated in itself, the Counterculture might have been too complex to support a simple image of it as a mere negation or dropping out. Viewed as a giant version of the amotivational syndrome, it was easier to understand and dismiss. The assessment of the amotivational syndrome was unassailable. It was unambiguously negative—loss of motivation, escape from reality, passivity. As a syndrome, moreover, it was a psychiatric condition with clear overtones of pathology. As the amotivational syndrome writ large, the Counterculture too appeared as unquestionably negative, and its negativity appeared as something specific and palpable—a mass psychiatric syndrome. The discrediting view of the Counterculture thus was reinforced by its association with marihuana, conceived as the source of the amotivational syndrome.

To restate this in a sentence: Marihuana functioned effectively as a cultural symbol. To use Clifford Geertz's terminology, it provided a template for organizing and making sense of a multitude of impressions of the Counterculture. It served as a "sensuous embodiment of what is abstract and ineffable" in Jaeger's and Selznick's phrase.[29]

The public images of drug and culture thus were mutually reinforcing. Because it symbolized a cultural phenomenon that was widely seen as a mere passive withdrawal from reality, marihuana use ceased to be seen primarily as a creator of violent criminals or as a stepping-stone to heroin and became instead a source of the amotivational syndrome. Because the Counterculture was symbolized by a "drop-out drug," its reputation as a pathological denial of society was made palpable and thus reinforced. Symbol and referent, marihuana and Counterculture, became confounded in public discussion.

NOTES

1. Earl Rowell and Robert Rowell, *On the Trail of Marihuana: The Weed of Madness* (Mountain View, Calif.: Pacific Press, 1939), p. 83.

2. "Pot Problem," *Time,* 12 March 1965, p. 49; Benjamin Spock, "Preventing Drug Abuse in Children," *Redbook,* May 1971, p. 36.

3. U.S., Senate, Committee on the Judiciary, *Narcotic Rehabilitation Act of 1966,* 89th Cong., 2d sess., 1966, p. 459.

4. U.S., House of Representatives, Committee on Interstate and Foreign Commerce, Subcommittee on Public Health and Welfare, *Increased Control Over Hallucinogens and Other Dangerous Drugs,* 90th Cong., 2d sess., 1968, pp. 101-103.

5. U.S., Senate, Committee on the Judiciary, *Juvenile Delinquency,* 90th Cong., 2d sess., 1968, pp. 4561, 4687; U.S., Senate, Committee on Labor and Public Welfare, Subcommittee on Alcoholism and Narcotics, *Narcotics Addiction and Drug Abuse,* 91st Cong., 1st sess., 1969, pp. 31-40, 95-100, 136, 197.

6. U.S., National Commission on Marihuana and Drug Abuse, *Marihuana: A Signal of Misunderstanding* (1972), p. 73.

7. "More Controversy About Pot," *Time,* 31 May 1971, p. 65.

8. Ibid.

9. U.S., Senate, Committee on the Judiciary, Subcommittee to Investigate the Administration of the Internal Security Act and Other Internal Security Laws, *Marihuana-Hashish Epidemic and Its Impact on United States Security,* 94th Cong., 1st sess., 1975.

10. National Commission, *Marihuana,* pp. 86-87.

11. The level of significance for the 1935-1940 vs. 1964-1976 comparison was greater than .05. The difference, however, was in the predicted direction. More importantly, references to passivity prior to the mid-1960s were perfunctory, and the effect was rarely said to be the distinguishing or central feature of the drug.

12. "Commonwealth vs. Leis and Weiss," in *Marihuana,* ed. Stanley Grupp (Columbus, Ohio: Charles E. Merrill, 1971), p. 295.

13. House of Representatives, *Hallucinogens,* p. 158.

14. The passages included here are the following: U.S., Senate, Committee on the Judiciary, Subcommittee to Investigate Juvenile Delinquency, *Narcotic Legislation,* 91st Cong., 1st sess., 1969, pp. 501, 516, 530-537, 571-609; U.S., Senate, Committee on Labor and Public Welfare, Special Committee on Alcoholism and Narcotics, *Federal Drug Abuse and Drug Dependence Prevention, Treatment, and Rehabilitation Act of 1970,* 91st Cong., 2d sess., 1970, p. 143; U.S., House of Representatives, Committee on Interstate and Foreign Commerce, Subcommittee on Public Health and Welfare, *Drug Abuse Control Amendments—1970,* 91st Cong., 2d sess., 1970, pp. 180-181, 188, 551-554; U.S., House of Representatives, Committee on Ways and Means, *Controlled Dangerous Substances, Narcotics, and Drug Control Laws,* 91st Cong., 2d sess., 1970, pp. 280ff., 331-334, 449. They include testimony from public health officials, the House Select Committee on Crime, the National Congress of Parents and Teachers, the 1969 Presidential Task Force on Narcotics, Marihuana, and Dangerous Drugs, the National Association of Retail Druggists, and others.

15. House of Representatives, *Controlled Dangerous Substances,* p. 280.

16. House of Representatives, *Drug Abuse Control Amendments,* p. 554.

17. National Commission, *Marihuana,* pp. 59, 61, 73, 79, 84-89.

18. Ibid., pp. 97, 99.

19. Senate, *Marihuana-Hashish Epidemic,* pp. 51, 193. The hearings included much testimony on the physiological and biochemical effects of marihuana as well.

20. Ibid., pp. 18-30, 154-169, 206-250.

21. Ibid., pp. 154-169, 206-250.

22. U.S., House of Representatives, Select Committee on Crime, *Crime in America—Drug Abuse and Criminal Justice,* 91st Cong., 1st sess., 1969, p. 172.

23. Senate, *Marihuana-Hashish Epidemic,* pp. 214, 232.

24. U.S., President's Ad Hoc Panel on Drug Abuse, *Progress Report* (Washington, D.C.: U.S. Government Printing Office, 1962); White House Conference on Narcotic and Drug Abuse, *Proceedings* (Washington, D.C.: U.S. Government Printing Office, 1962); U.S., President's Advisory Commission on Narcotic and Drug Abuse, *Final Report* (Washington, D.C.: U.S. Government Printing Office, 1963).

25. Gertrude Jaeger and Philip Selznick, "A Normative Theory of Culture," *American Sociological Review* 29 (1964):653-669.

26. S. K. Oberdeck, "Problems of Pot," *National Review,* 1 June 1971, p. 597.

27. Jeffrey Hart, "Marijuana and the Counter Culture," *National Review,* 8 December 1972, p. 1348.

28. National Commission, *Marihuana,* p. 167.

29. Clifford Geertz, "Ideology as a Cultural System," in *The Interpretation of Cultures* (New York: Basic Books, 1973), pp. 193-233; Jaeger and Selznick, "Normative Theory of Culture."

THE POLITICS AND IDEOLOGY OF DRUG CONTROL

8

We have examined the history of marihuana laws in the United States from the perspective of the four hypotheses presented in chapter 2 and looked closely at the changing terms in which marihuana has been publicly discussed. Let us now summarize the points we have made, looking first at each hypothesis and then at the general issue of the role of ideas in the history of the marihuana issue.

MARIHUANA BEFORE THE SIXTIES

From the mid-1930s until the early 1960s, the Federal Bureau of Narcotics played a dominant role in shaping public beliefs and state policy concerning marihuana. It effectively defined what was true about the drug and how it should be handled. When the bureau argued in the mid-1930s that marihuana had become a menace only recently, its assertion was repeated, often verbatim, in most public discussions. A few years later when it gave up the menace imagery, others soon followed suit. Those who discussed marihuana regarded it as a violence-inducing drug in the 1930s and as a stepping-stone to heroin in the 1950s largely because the bureau said it was. The impact of the LaGuardia Report in the 1940s was limited because the bureau successfully influenced the American Medical Association's response and defined what parts of the report received attention. At each point, most discussions of marihuana bore the mark of the bureau.

The FBN, however, did not wholly create the marihuana issue. When the bureau began to publicize the marihuana menace in the mid-1930s, marihuana already was a local issue—albeit a very minor one—in various parts of the country. Some states, primarily those in the West and Southwest, had passed laws against it; local law enforcement officials and politicians had complained occasionally to the federal government about it; various senators and congressmen had proposed federal marihuana legislation; and the drug had even made an occasional front-page newspaper headline. The bureau, moreover, drew upon an established image of marihuana. It did not originate the idea that marihuana use led to violence; it merely adopted the image of the "killer weed" from accounts of the drug in New Orleans and the Southwest.

In short, both the Anslinger Hypothesis and the Mexican Hypothesis have a modicum of validity. As the former assumes, the Federal Bureau of Narcotics did play an active, pivotal role in shaping marihuana beliefs and policy prior to the 1960s; as the latter argues, it did take up the marihuana issue from the West and Southwest. Fundamentally, however, neither hypothesis leads to a full understanding of the pre-1960s history of marihuana. Both the role of the bureau and the nature of local influence were far more complex and subtle than these hypotheses suggest.

The Anslinger Hypothesis

As I argued in chapter 2, the proponents of the Anslinger Hypothesis have rarely attempted to explain why the bureau pursued the marihuana issue. Those who have proposed explanations invariably have pictured the bureau as a moral crusader or a survival-conscious bureaucracy with a natural or obvious interest in taking on marihuana. Moral crusaders "naturally" seek to legislate morality; survival-conscious bureaucracies "naturally" seek to expand. In short, the proponents of the Anslinger Hypothesis have spent little time explaining why the bureau acted as it did because they have assumed that the question had a simple answer, that the issue was not problematic.

This assumption is the central and fatal flaw of most previous work on the bureau. In fact, the bureau had no obvious or natural interest in procuring national marihuana controls. To be sure, it was a survival-conscious bureaucracy and its leaders were moralists to the core, but neither fact predisposed it to seek control over marihuana or, for that matter, over barbiturates and amphetamines.

The bureau was not naturally aggressive or expansionistic. On the contrary, if it can be simply characterized at all, it was resolutely reticent. It perceived its own interests to lie in limiting the scope of its authority as much as possible. Chastened by low budgets, the problems of Prohibition, and the shaky judicial history of the Harrison Act, the newly created bureau in the early 1930s systematically sought to avoid adding new drugs to its purview and taking responsibility for day-to-day narcotics enforcement. Through the Uniform Narcotic Drugs Act, it attempted instead to make the states deal with marihuana and shoulder the general task of prosecuting narcotics users and small-time pushers. While it envisioned an eventual national marihuana law, it made no immediate effort to procure such legislation.

Once established, this pattern of resolute reticence persisted long after the precipitating conditions had disappeared. In the 1950s, when appropriations were plentiful, narcotics laws secure, and Prohibition but a memory, the bureau still was wary of added responsibilities. Commissioner Anslinger passionately rejected the offer of barbiturate control on at least three separate occasions.

The bureau's decisions first to play up the evils of marihuana in late 1934 and then to seek a national law about a year later were the unintended and paradoxical consequences of its avoidance strategy. With the Uniform Act failing to gain state adoption, the bureau turned to the specter of marihuana to persuade recalcitrant legislators that the act was important. The added attention to marihuana may have triggered a new set of congressional proposals for a national marihuana law in 1935, which in turn was the occasion for the Treasury Department to overrule the bureau's reticence and order it to draft national legislation.

When the bureau found itself in the position of seeking a national marihuana law, it proceeded with moralistic gusto because it did regard the drug as an evil and had no moral reservations against adding marihuana prohibition to the federal books. The Marihuana Tax Act, however, was not the result of a simple moralistic or expansionist impulse.

The Anslinger Hypothesis also takes for granted the bureau's

success in procuring the Marihuana Tax Act and dominating marihuana policy for over twenty-five years. There has been little discussion of how the bureau managed to prevail. Its success, as well
as its motivation, has been taken as natural and inevitable.

Again, the social reality is more complex. The bureau's success
was based on certain social conditions, and when those conditions
changed, its dominance was shaken. Prior to the 1960s, the bureau
was able to dominate public discussion of marihuana because the
drug was an insignificant issue; no other would-be moral entrepreneurs took a major interest in it, and users were socially marginal
and powerless. As use exploded and spread to the middle class
in the 1960s, marihuana became a major public issue. A growing
list of organizations and interest groups became concerned with the
marihuana problem; the larger, better-heeled user constituency
effectively mobilized; and the general public became deeply involved. The number of forces seeking to define the marihuana
issue increased, as did the sources of information about the drug.
Individual citizens not only had a diverse array of reputable experts upon whom to call but also had better access to users themselves. The sheer size and diversity of public discussion doomed
the narcotics officials' monopoly over the marihuana issue.

The loss of hegemony is clear. Although narcotics officials remained a potent force in the marihuana arena, they no longer
successfully defined issues. In the later 1960s, narcotics officials
argued that marihuana was truly dangerous, but the dominant
view was that the dangers had been exaggerated. They claimed
that marihuana users became violent, but the amotivational syndrome
became the effect most commonly imputed to the drug; they ada-
mantly opposed any reduction in penalties, but those reductions
came anyway. The 1970s found narcotics officials moderating
their danger argument, adopting the amotivational syndrome claim,
and giving up active opposition to penalty reduction.

The errors of the Anslinger Hypothesis point to two general
lessons about the behavior of formal organizations and the dynamics
of moral entrepreneurship. First, formal organizations are not
invariably expansionistic or imperialistic. They may adopt any of a
number of survival strategies, of which expansion is but one. Second,
moral entrepreneurs do not exist in a vacuum. The success of a
paarticular organization in defining and dominating a social problem

depends not only on its own efforts but also on the nature of its social context.

The Mexican Hypothesis

The Mexican Hypothesis has argued that anti-Mexican sentiment in the Southwest in the late 1920s and early 1930s led to intense concern about marihuana use, which caused local officials to complain to the federal government. These complaints in turn pressured the bureau into seeking a national marihuana law.

As we have seen, this argument is weak at several points. Although there was widespread anti-Mexican sentiment in the Southwest during the time in question, marihuana was an insignificant issue in anti-Mexican movements and on its own. Although there clearly was some pressure on federal officials, it was intermittent and spread over more than twenty years. The bureau's response to this pressure, moreover, was not to seek a national law but to deny that such a law was necessary and to urge state action instead. Finally, by the time the bureau began to talk about a marihuana menace and to seek federal legislation, the image of the violent Mexican user had been replaced in public discussion by that of the youthful victim. The Marihuana Tax Act was justified primarily as a way of saving youth, not as a way of punishing Mexicans.

Although the Marihuana Tax Act was in no sense an anti-Mexican law, the association of marihuana with Mexican laborers and other lower-class groups still influenced marihuana beliefs and policy in less direct ways. The act was justified with the argument that marihuana was a menace. Marihuana was said to be a menace because it made its users violent—it was a "killer weed"—and because it was spreading to or "infecting" the youth of America. These perceptions of the drug, however, were shaped decisively by the social locus of use. The "killer weed" image originated in New Orleans and the Southwest, where marihuana was associated with Mexican laborers and other lower-class groups. These groups were perceived to be criminal and violent, and thus marihuana gained a reputation for creating crime and violence. Because these using groups were also socially disreputable and distant from the mainstream of society, marihuana was perceived as an "alien" and inimical force. Its alleged spread to youth, therefore, appeared as an "infection."

In short, marihuana was condemned and proscribed not because it was used by Mexicans, but because it was a "killer weed" infecting youth. The images of "killer weed" and "infection," however, were shaped by the drug's association with Mexican laborers and other lower-class groups. The relationship between Mexicans and the Marihuana Tax Act thus was mediated by a particular image of the drug. Only when marihuana became unambiguously associated with middle-class youth in the 1960s did the image fundamentally change.

The Mexican Hypothesis fails because it rests upon too simple a notion of the relationship between the social class of the user and the legal status of the drug—a flaw that it shares with much of the drug control literature. It treats the actual terms in which drug laws are discussed and justified as mere smokescreens that hide the real social forces at work and hence that merit little attention. It thus does not see that the social class of the drug user can influence the legal status of the drug by shaping these terms of discussion. In other words, it does not appreciate the importance of ideology.

MARIHUANA SINCE THE SIXTIES

The middle-class social position and the Countercultural affiliation of many marihuana users during the late 1960s and early 1970s had a significant impact on public discussion of marihuana and on the law, but this impact was more complex than suggested by either the Embourgeoisement Hypothesis or the Hippie Hypothesis.

The Embourgeoisement Hypothesis

Marihuana certainly has not become as American as apple pie. Far from it: It does not have (and probably will never have) the moral acceptability or the legal availability of alcohol, let alone coffee or tea. The dangers of use continue to be hotly debated. Nonetheless, the changes in public discussion that have occurred are quite significant.

During the 1960s and 1970s, for the first time, marihuana appeared as a less than wholly dangerous and disreputable drug. Its dangers were discounted by some, and more importantly the possibility of moderate, controlled, nonabusive use was widely accepted.

Marihuana no longer appeared as intrinsically, inevitably evil. Condemnation of use was no longer totally automatic. At the same time, a consensus developed in favor of a *de facto* decriminalization. Beyond the considerable support for the formal reduction or removal of criminal penalties for use, there was even wider agreement that ideally no one should go to jail simply for using the drug. Marihuana thus gained a quasi-legitimacy.

These changes were partly the result of the diffusion of marihuana into the middle class; however, the impact of the changed social locus of use on public discussion of the drug occurred in a complex set of ways. We have distinguished three different causal pathways. First, marihuana users themselves became a political force in the drug control arena. They not only constituted an organized, articulate group that exerted pressure for marihuana law reform but also provided a suitable audience for public health officials, intellectuals, and others who were predisposed to challenge existing beliefs and policy. Second, the dominant images of marihuana users (as users) changed dramatically. They appeared as ''someone's kids,'' not as anonymous users; as fundamentally normal persons who happened to commit deviant acts, not as deviant persons; and as persons whose opinions on marihuana deserved a hearing. In each case, the changed image of the users provided an impetus for policymakers and the media to pay attention to positive information about marihuana use. As a result, the drug became seen as less dangerous, and an important argument in favor of harsh penalties was undermined. Third, a number of new arguments in favor of marihuana law reform gained prominence. Harsh penalties for marihuana users were opposed on the grounds that users were not ''really'' criminals, despite their drug use; that the existing law was not credible to the users themselves and thus lacked deterrent force; and that a felony marihuana conviction could ruin the users' careers and lives. These arguments were important in winning support for penalty reductions.

The reevaluation of marihuana and the reform of marihuana laws thus did not result wholly from the entry of newly created promarihuana interests and groups into the drug control arena. It stemmed as well from changes in the ideology of the marihuana issue in the conceptual framework of public discussion. The emergence of middle-class marihuana use altered the tacit, taken-for-granted assumptions about the user and the law. These new assumptions in turn were hospitable to a benign view of the drug and to support for marihuana law reform. One did not need to be a marihuana user or the parent of a user—one did not need, in other words, to have a direct interest in the matter—to take a liberal stand on the drug. One merely needed to imbibe the changed ideology, to participate in the new culture, of the marihuana issue. The changed ideological framework insinuated itself much more broadly than the reach of mere self-interest and was responsible for the surprisingly wide acknowledgment of moderate use and support for law reform. In short, as in the case of the Mexican Hypothesis, ideology was a crucial mediating link between the social locus of the user and the legal status of the drug.

The Hippie Hypothesis

Marihuana became a symbol—an embodiment—of the Counterculture in the late 1960s and early 1970s for policymakers and the media as well as for rebellious youth. The drug's symbolic role was sometimes explicitly acknowledged, and occasionally the drug was condemned for the lifestyle and values it symbolized, rather than for its effects. The main result of marihuana's symbolic status, however, lay not in transferring attention from the drug's effects to what it represented but in transforming how those effects themselves were conceptualized.

Disapproval of marihuana was justified most commonly by reference not to the threat posed by the Counterculture to the dominant society but to the harm that marihuana allegedly was doing to its users. The way that this harm was conceptualized, however, clearly reflected marihuana's symbolic embodiment of the Counterculture. Where marihuana once had been accused of destroying its users's restraint and making them violent, it was now condemned for destroying their motivation and making them passive and withdrawn. This new claim was simply the popular image of the Counterculture projected onto marihuana, individualized, and reduced to a psychiatric diagnosis. Once established, the image of marihuana as a "drop-out drug" served as a template for organizing perceptions of the more diffuse, harder to comprehend Counterculture.

The symbolic relationship between marihuana and the Counterculture, in short, was more subtle and had a more complex effect on public discussion than is envisioned in the Hippie Hypothesis.

Perceptions of the symbol and its referent mutually shaped each other.

The social background and cultural affiliation of the marihuana user, of course, were not the only factors shaping public discussion and the law in the late 1960s and early 1970s. The vastly increased number of users in itself probably was important. A small group of users, no matter how high their social position, would have been less effective as a political actor or audience; fewer policymakers, media writers, and middle-class parents would have had direct accessibility to users or an interest in their fate; the credibility of the law to users and the impact of punishment on their careers probably would have been less significant issues.

Similarly, the presence of reputable experts willing to give concrete formulation and scientific legitimacy to certain new beliefs about marihuana was no doubt crucial. Without them the feelings of marihuana users and concerned parents might have remained inchoate and unvalidated. The public health and medical affiliations of many of these experts, moreover, probably influenced the recasting of marihuana's harmful effects from violence (a public safety concern) to the amotivational syndrome (a public health concern).

Finally, the nature of the drug itself played a definite role. Marihuana, as we have noted, has no spectacularly negative short-term effects. If it had such effects, the massive increase in middle-class use would have resulted in equally massive, undeniable pathology, and the middle-class social background of the users would have stimulated, rather than muted, panic.

None of these factors, however, negates the importance of social background and cultural affiliation. The effects of marihuana were no different in the 1930s than in the 1960s. Reputable experts, willing to downplay the dangers of marihuana, had been available well before the mid-1960s. A vast increase in marihuana use limited to ghetto blacks and barrio Chicanos hardly would have led to the myriad changes in stereotypes, political forces, and arguments that actually resulted in the reform of marihuana laws and the reformulation of its dangers.

TAKING IDEOLOGY SERIOUSLY

Throughout our discussion, we have been concerned with ideology in a broad sense—the framework of taken-for-granted beliefs, perceptions, and assumptions within which marihuana and the laws controlling it have been publicly discussed. Our attention has focused on how the image of the drug changed from a "killer weed" in the 1930s into a "drop-out drug" in the 1960s. Ideology has also figured importantly in our evaluation of the four marihuana hypotheses.

We have examined how the public discussion of marihuana has been framed or structured; how this conceptual framework has been socially shaped by moral entrepreneurs, the social locus of use, and broader social conflicts; and how it in turn has helped to determine the nature of marihuana laws. We have, in other words, treated ideology as an important mediating factor in the social shaping of marihuana laws. We thus have taken ideology seriously by treating it not as a mere mask that hides the real social forces at work but as an integral part of those social forces.

Taking ideology seriously, however, does not mean regarding ideas as wholly autonomous, independent forces. To the contrary, we have tried to show the social and historical rootedness of the conceptions that have framed public discussion of marihuana. We can conclude our analysis by addressing more directly the issue of the independent role of ideas.

Consider the following alternative explanation of some of the changes in beliefs about marihuana described in this study: Perhaps beliefs about marihuana are decisively shaped simply by the available information about the drug. From this perspective, the rise of the amotivational syndrome claim and the tendency to downplay the dangers of marihuana in the 1960s can be seen as the products of new information on the drug. With the proliferation of studies on marihuana, it perhaps became clear that moderate use was possible and that the drug's main effect was passivity, not violence. The implication here is that certain ideas about marihuana developed more or less independently of the social forces described in this study.

A simple way of gauging the impact of information is to note that the two major claims about the effects of marihuana—the pre-1960s violence argument and the more recent amotivational syndrome argument—both came to prominence on the basis of minimal evidence. As noted in chapter 4, the bureau provided little support for its assertion that marihuana caused violence. At the 1937 House hearings on the Marihuana Tax Act, it offered one briefly summarized study of prisoners, some time-honored

Old World legends, and a half dozen examples of allegedly marihuana-related crimes. At the same time, it ignored or downplayed
those studies that contradicted the violence claim.

The amotivational syndrome claim of the 1960s and 1970s originated with only slightly better support. Consider, for example,
the evidence offered at the 1974 marihuana-hashish hearings, which
were called by Senator Eastland just to publicize the dangers of
marihuana. Support for the claim that marihuana use systematically
caused an amotivational syndrome was based solely on observation of clinical populations. No data on general populations were
presented, and there was no discussion of the well-known problems
of generalizing from clinical data. The observations of clinical
populations, moreover, were largely unsystematic: Harvey Powelson
(University of California, Berkeley, Student Health Service), Henry
Brill (New York State Department of Mental Hygiene), and John
Hall (Kingston Hospital, Jamaica) all referred to their clinical
experience in an offhand, anecdotal way.[1] Hardin Jones (University of California, Berkeley) claimed to have interviewed some
1,600 marihuana users and to have seen "some degree of amotivational syndrome in all of them."[2] He mentioned no control group,
however; nor did he specify the composition and source of his
sample, the nature and extent of the interviews, or the criteria used
to identify the amotivational syndrome. Jones, moreover, was
trained as a physicist and physiologist, not as a psychiatrist or
psychologist. This leaves the testimony of Harold Kolansky and
William Moore, two Philadelphia psychiatrists, who studied thirty-
eight marihuana users in the course of their private practices. They
claimed that all of their marihuana-using patients showed an amotivational syndrome quite distinct from anything exhibited by their
nonusing patients and that this syndrome disappeared when marihuana use was discontinued.[3] Their study is certainly more rigorous
than the other evidence cited at the hearing, but even if we accept
its findings at face value, there is no basis for inferring the prevalence
of an amotivational syndrome among the general population of
marihuana users.

The lack of evidence for both the violence and the amotivational
syndrome claims leads us to a more general point. Information
in itself has rarely played an independent or direct role in shaping
marihuana ideology. Its impact has been mediated by the various

social forces already described in this study. To understand how this is so, let us first distinguish two kinds of available information, scientific information, which is systematically gathered in a planned, self-conscious way, and practical information, which is the byproduct of everyday experience. In other words, knowledge about marihuana may be based either on specially designed studies of varying methodological sophistication or on contact with the drug and its users in the course of everyday life.

Access to either scientific or practical information on marihuana has been shaped by a number of social conditions. At any time few persons have comprehensive firsthand knowledge of the scientific literature on marihuana. Policymakers, the media, and the general populace have relied on the reports of "reputable experts," those who successfully claim expertise concerning marihuana. The impact of scientific information on marihuana beliefs thus has been mediated by a structure of information control.

Prior to the 1960s, the Federal Bureau of Narcotics virtually monopolized the dissemination of scientific information on marihuana, and it publicized and gave credence to only that material consistent with its view of the drug. As a result, much of the available scientific information, including much of the methodologically soundest, was either ignored or discredited. The 1894 Indian Hemp Commission Report, the 1925 and 1932 Canal Zone studies, Walter Bromberg's 1934 crime study, and the LaGuardia Report all received little or biased attention.

Since the mid-1960s, the structure of information control has changed significantly. The vast explosion of scientific information on marihuana and its growing methodological sophistication has made policymakers, the media, and the general populace all the more reliant on reputable experts. At the same time, the variety of these experts has increased. No one agency monopolizes the dissemination of information. There is instead a plurality of sources that often disagree on the basic issues of how dangerous marihuana is and what its specific effects are. Those seeking scientific information must decide whom to believe: Should they follow those who describe marihuana as a dangerous weed or those who call it a mild euphoriant; should they agree with those who say it causes an amotivational syndrome or those who deny that it does? In such circumstances the effect of scientific information on marihuana beliefs is mediated not only by the structure of information control but also by the predispositions of the lay public. It is plausible that policymakers, media writers, and the general populace decide which experts to believe (and thus which scientific information to accept) on the basis of their own practical experience.

Opportunities for practical experience with marihuana, especially for policymakers and the media, however, have depended on the prevalence and social locus of use. Prior to the 1960s, when marihuana use was limited to relatively few persons from lower-class and culturally marginal groups, neither policymakers nor the media had much opportunity for direct contact with users or the drug itself. They thus had no practical knowledge and no personal basis for evaluating the scientific information provided them. With the proliferation of middle-class marihuana use in the mid-1960s, however, possibilities for practical knowledge abounded. Policymakers and media writers could readily observe in natural settings persons who had used marihuana and could even smoke the stuff themselves. They thus could gather practical information on the drug. Some might have been convinced by their personal experience that marihuana was indeed a dangerous drug. Many, however, decided that the marihuana users they had listened to and observed were basically normal persons and that the drug was really not very dangerous. They were thus predisposed to accept those reports of scientific information that downplayed the harmfulness of the drug.

Information therefore has influenced marihuana ideology and law only as it has been filtered through a structure of information control and through the predispositions of policymakers, the media, and the general populace. Both of these in turn have been shaped by the very social factors we have already discussed. This returns us to the basic point: While ideas have played an important role in the history of marihuana control in the United States, the role has been socially structured, not wholly independent.

NOTES

1. U.S., Senate, Committee on the Judiciary, Subcommittee to Investigate the Administration of the Internal Security Act and Other Internal Security Laws, *Marihuana-Hashish Epidemic and Its Impact on United States Security*, 94th Cong., 1st sess., 1974, pp. 18-36, 147-154.

2. Ibid., p. 232.

3. Ibid., pp. 154-169.

METHODOLOGICAL APPENDIX

The present study has two important methodological features. First, it is comparative. It does not merely describe the historical development of marihuana law and ideology; it systematically compares what was said about marihuana at various times. This allows us to determine what was truly distinctive about marihuana ideology at any given point. Second, the study includes a quantitative content analysis of periodical articles to show that the historical picture of marihuana ideology it presents is indeed representative of what was said about marihuana at various times. This analysis allows us to document, for example, that violence was the effect most often imputed to marihuana in the 1930s not only with selected quotes (the representativeness of which much be accepted as given) but also with the statistical datum that x percent of articles from the 1930s mentioned violence compared to only y percent in the 1960s. The result is a much more systematic, rigorous account of marihuana ideology than otherwise possible.

Data used in this study comes from periodical articles indexed in the *Readers' Guide to Periodical Literature* (RG) and from a variety of other primary sources. The *Readers' Guide* materials have two uses: First, the relative frequency of articles on marihuana in the RG provides a measure of the magnitude of the marihuana issue over the years. Second, a content analysis of these articles gives us a representative picture of what was said about the drug. We shall call these the "magnitude study" and the "content study" respectively. Data from other primary sources are used to reinforce, refine, or modify the conclusions reached from the RG data.

READERS' GUIDE DATA

The *Readers' Guide to Periodical Literature* is the major index of articles appearing in general-interest periodicals in the United States. A successor to such nineteenth-century publications as *Poole's Index to Periodical Literature,* it has been published by the H. W. Wilson Company since 1900 with the assistance of the American Library Association (ALA). There is even a retrospective volume for the 1890s. Bound volumes of the RG initially appeared every five years, but the intervals have gradually decreased to one year. The RG has consistently sought to index major periodicals of a broad, general, and popular nature. The list of articles is selected by a vote of subscribers, supervised by the ALA Committee on Wilson Indexes, and revised at intervals to add new titles and drop others. In effect, then, the RG indexes those periodicals judged by major librarians to be the most useful and important. Despite the continual addition and deletion of titles, the RG is generally judged to have maintained a fairly constant scope throughout its existence.

Within this general consistency, there have been a number of changes in emphasis and content. Among other things, the number of periodicals indexed has increased continually from 66 in volume 1 (1900-1904) to 118 in volume 12 (1939-1941), 132 in volume 23 (1961-1963), and about 160 in recent volumes. This means that the total number of articles indexed has risen. The 1900-1904 volume contains 574 pages per year; the 1925-1928 volume, 702 pages; the 1937-1939 volume, 1,020 pages; the 1945-1947 volume, 1,138 pages; and the 1955-1957 volume, 1,385 pages. In subsequent years, the annual number of pages has remained fairly constant, the 1974-1975 volume containing 1,232 pages per year. Furthermore, the RG initially indexed books, government publications, and the annual reports of intellectual associations in addition to periodical articles. Books were discontinued after volume 3 (1910-1914), and the reports and government publications gradually dwindled. Subsequent to a 1952 ALA-sponsored policy change, scholarly publications (for example, *The American Journal of Sociology*) were transferred from the RG to the *International Index,* which was begun in 1913 as a supplement to the RG and currently appears in two volumes as the *Social Science Index* and the *Humanities Index.* An effort was made to reserve the RG for publications of more general interest; therefore, periodicals for specialists or for specific hobbies were explicitly excluded.[1]

In short, the major changes in the content of the RG since 1900 have been an increase in the number of periodicals covered, a gradual decrease in nonperiodical material, and the exclusion of scholarly and highly specialized periodicals. The first of these changes occasionally must be kept in mind in analyzing the data from the magnitude study. For example, since the RG contained about 20 percent more articles in the early 1970s than in the late 1930s (1,232 pages vs. 1,020 pages), a mere 20 percent increase in the annual frequency of marihuana articles in the later period over the earlier period would not indicate that more attention was being given to marihuana relative to other issues.

The other changes do not seem to affect our findings in any way. Nonperiodical material never constituted more than a small fraction of the entries in the RG, and the exclusion of scholarly publications in 1952 does not appear to have caused any abrupt change in the frequency or content of articles on marihuana.

The Magnitude Study

Variations in the frequencies of articles on marihuana and alcohol that are indexed in the *Readers' Guide to Periodical Literature* from 1890 to 1976 are used as indicators of the relative amount of attention given marihuana during various time periods. Assessments of the relative importance of the marihuana issue are based on comparisons of the frequency of articles on marihuana at a particular time with both the frequency of articles on alcohol at the same time period and the frequencies of articles on marihuana at other periods.

This methodology need not assume that the frequency of articles in the RG at any one time is an accurate indicator of the magnitude of the marihuana issue at the same time. Rather, since the analysis is comparative, it must make the somewhat less exacting assumption that the relationship between the article frequency in the RG and the magnitude of the issue in broader public discussion remains constant over time.

A count was made of articles in the RG on alcohol and marihuana. Included among the alcohol articles were all those indexed in the following categories: alcohol, alcoholics, alcoholism, alcohol and youth, alcohol and servicemen, alcohol education, liquor laws, liquor problem, liquor traffic, Prohibition, and temperance. Marihuana articles included those indexed under the marihuana, cannabis, hashish, and THC headings.

In hoosing the alcohol categories, an effort was made to include all and only those articles that appeared to discuss the substance either as a social problem or as a matter of scientific interest. Articles under those headings concerning alcohol as a beverage or the alcoholic beverage industry were excluded, because a brief survey of titles showed them to be oriented to the alcohol consumer (that is, how to mix better drinks) or investor (that is, how to invest wisely in the industry), not to a discussion of alcohol as a social problem or matter of scientific interest.

The annual frequencies of articles on alcohol and marihuana were computed for each time period covered by a volume of the RG. The follow-·ꞑg ratios were then calculated to allow for comparison:

1. *marihuana/alcohol ratio:* the ratio of the annual frequency of articles on marihuana to the annual frequency of articles on alcohol for each time period.

2. *marihuana/1967-76 mean:* the ratio of the annual frequency of articles on marihuana for each time period prior to 1967 to the average annual frequency of articles on marihuana from 1967 to 1976 (31.4).

The use of these ratios is straightforward, given the assumptions we have made. The larger the marihuana/alcohol ratio for any time period, the greater the amount of attention given marihuana relative to alcohol at the time. The larger the marihuana/1967-76 mean ratio, the closer the amount of attention given marihuana in a pre-1967 time period comes to approximating the amount of attention given the drug in the late 1960s and early 1970s, a period in which marihuana was irrefutably an important issue. Both ratios thus provide a measure of the relative importance of marihuana as a public issue at any given time.

The Content Study

Periodical articles on marihuana are studied to determine what beliefs about the drug have been presented in the printed media. Periodical, rather than newspaper, articles are used for two reasons. First, periodical articles are more accessible, since a wide range of periodicals are indexed in the RG. In contrast, hardly any newspapers besides the *New York Times* are indexed for more than a decade or two. Second, newspaper accounts of marihuana use usually report specific arrests or seizures rather than generally discussing the drug. They are thus not suited for our inquiry.

The sample of articles was taken from the marihuana, THC, hashish, and cannabis categories in the *Readers' Guide* from 1890 to 1976. Articles indexed under "hemp," mostly from the early 1900s, were ignored because they invariably concerned the production of hemp for rope, hempseed, and hemp oil and thus did not discuss the psychoactive uses of the plant.

The initial sample consisted of all articles in the four categories from 1890 to 1966 (N = 56) and a random selection of one-fifth of the articles from 1967 to 1976 (N = 65). The latter group actually turned out to be slightly more than 20 percent of the 314 articles indexed during the decade. The limited selection of articles after 1966 was necessary because the frequency of articles on marihuana increased sharply at the time, as noted in chapter 3.

The articles were read to determine whether or not they expressed or reported opinions on the following items:

1. *Degree of Danger:* How dangerous is marihuana?

2. *Possibility of Moderate Use:* Is moderate (that is, limited, safe) use possible?

3. *Effects:* What kinds of harm does marihuana use cause to users and those around them?
4. *Users:* From which social groups is the typical marihuana user drawn?

Items one through three are central to any characterization of marihuana. "Degree of danger" is probably the most important explicit issue in any public discussion of drug use. The belief that a drug can be used in moderate doses without ill effect, whatever the danger of heavier use, has been crucial in the differential perception of narcotic and nonnarcotic drugs. Central to the American condemnation of "narcotics" has been the argument that their use invariably leads to abuse, while the contemporary defense of alcohol is that despite the clear danger of protracted use, moderate use clearly can be distinguished from abuse. Finally, the specific effects imputed to marihuana have changed strikingly over time and thus constitute an important variable in the drug's image. Item four helps to indicate how public perceptions of who uses marihuana have developed. All four items are relevant to our assessment of the hypotheses presented in chapter 2 and to our examination of marihuana ideology.

Fourteen of the articles in the periodical sample provided no data on any of the four items and were excluded from further study. Eleven were reports from *Science* on efforts to isolate the active constituents of marihuana or on observations of the effects of marihuana on nonhuman animals. The three others included a history of marihuana with no references to the twentieth century, a 1969 report of Mexican efforts to crack down on marihuana cultivation, and a defense of the Consumer Union's 1972 drug report. A fifteenth article was removed because it turned out to be a series of letters to the editor that expressed a variety of viewpoints and hence could not be easily coded. The deletions reduced the actual sample N to 106—47 from the 1890-1963 period and 59 from the 1964-1976 period.[2]

As Table 13 shows, the articles appeared in a wide range of publications and included a disproportionate number from popular and professional science journals. The most represented publications were *Time* (eleven), *Science* (ten), *Newsweek* (ten), *Science News Letter* (ten), *Scientific American* (five), and *Science Digest* (five). The particular publication or kind of publication in which an article appeared generally had little effect on how marihuana was characterized in regard to the items relevant here.

Articles were read and coded for the opinions they expressed on each of the four items. The coding criteria were these:

1. *Degree of Danger.* An article was said to describe marihuana as "dangerous" if it explicitly referred to use as a "menace," "peril," or "problem" or if it paid preponderant attention to at least some of the negative effects of

Table 13
CONTENT STUDY SAMPLE, DISTRIBUTION BY SOURCE
(N = 106)

Periodical	Articles	Periodical	Articles
American Libraries	1	Literary Digest	3
American Magazine	1	Living Age	1
American Mercury	2	Look	1
American Scholar	1	Mademoiselle	1
Asia	1	Nation	1
Atlantic Monthly	1	National Review	3
Business Week	2	Nature	1
Christian Century	3	New Republic	2
Collier's	1	N. Y. Times Magazine	1
Commentary	1	New Yorker	1
Commonweal	1	Newsweek	10
Consumer Reports	1	Popular Science	2
Cornhill Magazine	1	Reader's Digest	1
Cosmopolitan	1	Redbook	1
Current	1	Science	10
Dun's	1	Science Digest	5
Forbes	1	Science News Letter	10
Forum and Century	1	Scientific American	5
Good Housekeeping	2	Senior Scholastic	1
Harper's	1	Spectator	1
Hygeia (Family Health)	3	Survey Graphic	1
Journal of Home Economics	1	Time	11
Life	2	U.S. News & World Report	2

the drug. An article was classified as describing marihuana as "not so dangerous" if it explicitly denied that use was a problem, de-emphasized or questioned reported dangers, or paid preponderant attention to the harmlessness
or the positive uses of the drug. In all, fifty-three articles were classified as
"dangerous," thirty-five as "not so dangerous," and the remaining eighteen
as expressing no opinion.

    2. *Possibility of Moderate Use.* An article was said to assert that moderate
use was "impossible" if it explicitly said that using marihuana even once or
twice was dangerous or if it described any condition that would make limited,
safe use impossible. These conditions included addiction, which implies that

the user is likely to lose control over use; subtlety of danger, which implies that negative effects occur without the user realizing them; immediacy of danger, which implies that negative effects (violence, acute psychotic reaction) can occur after even one use; and unpredictability of effect, which implies that users have no way of predicting effects and thus limiting their use accordingly. In contrast, an article was said to describe moderate use as "possible" if it explicitly stated that marihuana could be used one or more times without ill effect, if it distinguished "experimental," "social," or "weekend" use from heavier use, or if it compared marihuana favorably to drugs like alcohol, the moderate use of which is generally deemed possible. Twenty-five articles were classified as "impossible," thirty-nine as "possible," and forty-two as expressing no opinion.

3. *Effects.* An article was coded for each effect that it reported that marihuana had on the user and/or on others. Effects were categorized as follows:

violence—violent crimes against self or others (homicide, rape, robbery, suicide) or the predisposition to commit such acts.

passivity—loss of ability or desire to participate in the world; heightened desire to escape or withdraw.

addiction—physical dependence (tolerance and/or withdrawal symptoms).

dependence—psychological or emotional habituation without physical dependence.

stepping-stone—progression to more dangerous drugs.

debauchery—socially disapproved erotic activity.

accidents—impaired psychomotor abilities leading to motor vehicle accidents.

unpredictability—no consistent pattern of effects.

miscellaneous acute effects—unspecified or numerous immediate effects.

miscellaneous chronic effects—general long-term debilitation.

In all, eighty-five articles mentioned at least one effect of marihuana use.

4. *Users.* Fifty-nine of the articles referred to social groups believed to be the predominant users of marihuana. Articles were coded for each group mentioned according to the following categories: (1) Mexicans and other Spanish-speaking groups; (2) blacks; (3) bohemians and aesthetes; (4) hippies and rebels; (5) other marginal groups (East Indians, Orientals, criminals, the "idle and dissolute"); (6) youth in general (teenagers, adolescents, high-school students); (7) youth of the upper and middle strata (college students, middle-class youth, prep school students, children of professionals, politicians, and businessmen); (8) adults of the upper and middle strata (suburbanites, businessmen, professionals); (9) musicians and writers. The first five categories, which consist of groups that historically have been socially marginal in some sense, were also combined into a larger, "marginal" caregory; groups six through eight were combined into a larger, "respectable" category. In this way, groups

likely to be perceived as inherently immoral were distinguished from those that
would not. "Musicians and writers," rarely mentioned in any case, were left
out as ambiguous.

Articles that reported the belief of a person other than the author were
coded as though they had expressed the belief directly if they did not offer
substantial criticism or cite contrary evidence. Thus a 1970 *Time* report of
John Kaplan's argument that marihuana was relatively innocuous was coded
as describing marihuana as "not so dangerous" since it cited his position
at length and mentioned criticisms only as amending, not refuting, his case.
Similarly, a 1974 *Newsweek* report of Robert Kolodny's finding that marihuana use reduced testosterone levels in men was coded as describing marihuana as "dangerous" since it offered no contrary arguments and described
the study as a "jolt to pot smokers."[3]

Tabulations were made for each item for the 1890-1963 and 1964-1976
periods as well as for the 1935-1940 subperiod. 1964 was taken as a convenient cutting point, since the first drugs-on-campus, drugs-in-the-suburbs
articles appeared in that year, heralding the rise of middle-class marihuana
use. The 1935-1940 subperiod, which included the passage of the Marihuana Tax Act, was singled out, because it represented the height of concern over marihuana in the pre-1964 period. The tabulations allow for a
general characterization of each period and for comparisons between
periods. Such comparisons were made between 1964-1976 and both 1890-
1963 and 1935-1940, using Chi square modified by Yates's correction for
continuity as a test of significance. This statistical analysis gives us a clear
sense of the distinctiveness of marihuana beliefs in each time period.

Articles categorized as expressing no opinion on a particular item were
excluded from the statistical analyses of that item. Percentage calculations
were based on the number of cases expressing a clear opinion (the Relevant
N referred to in the various tables in the text), not on the total number of
cases. This may seem a questionable move since it removes from eighteen
to forty-seven cases, depending on the item. It makes sense, however,
when we realize that the high number of "no opinions" reflects nothing
more than the narrow focus of many of the articles. Some articles report
on marihuana use among a particular group without discussing effects.
Others discuss effects without mentioning specific users. Still others discuss
the magnitude of danger without specifying either effects or users. Depending on the focus of the article, some matters are relevant, others are not.
The high rate of missing data reflects nothing more profound than this
simple fact. Given this problem, one could have simply restricted the sample
to general, all-inclusive articles on marihuana, but that would have excluded
the vast majority of articles in the sample and removed many valuable bits

of data. Instead it was decided to include for each item only those articles from the sample that addressed the item with the recognition that the Relevant N thus created differed somewhat from item to item.

DATA FROM OTHER PRIMARY SOURCES

A variety of other primary sources are cited in this study to augment the findings of the RG studies. The most important of these are various federal government documents.

Congressional hearings and federal reports on psychoactive drug use are used to study marihuana ideology as it directly influenced and was used to justify changes in the law. A list of major hearings and reports was compiled from the major histories of American drug controls and from several anthologies.[4] The reports include material from the 1931 Wickersham Commission volume, entitled *Report on Crime and the Foreign Born,* the 1956 interdepartmental committee on narcotics, a series of inquiries into "narcotics and drug abuse" commissioned by President Kennedy in the early 1960s, President Johnson's 1966 crime commission, the 1972 marihuana report of the National Commission of Marihuana and Drug Abuse, and the annual assessments of marihuana and health by the Department of Health, Education, and Welfare. Included among the hearings are the 1937 House and Senate hearings on the Marihuana Tax Act, the various hearings on the 1951 Boggs Act and the Narcotics Control Act of 1956, the 1950 Kefauver organized crime hearings, various mid-1960s hearings on LSD and marihuana, the numerous hearings on the Comprehensive Drug Abuse Prevention and Control Act of 1970, the Eastland subcommittee's 1974 hearings on the so-called marihuana-hashish epidemic, and the 1975 hearings on marihuana decriminalization.

The annual reports of the Federal Bureau of Narcotics (*Traffic in Opium and Other Dangerous Drugs*) from 1926 to 1962 were examined to facilitate our understanding of the vicissitudes of the bureau's stance toward marihuana and its role in shaping marihuana ideology and law. This time period was chosen to cover the heyday of the bureau's control over federal drug policy—from the bureau's creation in 1930 to the retirement of Commissioner Harry Anslinger in 1962. With the election of John F. Kennedy and his establishment of a White House conference and a presidential commission to study narcotics and drug abuse, drug policy became a wider government concern and ceased to be the relatively private domain of any one federal agency.[5] The marihuana ideology of federal narcotics officials after 1962 was studied along with those of other policymakers through testimony at congressional hearings as well as through official pamphlets and speeches.

NOTES

1. The discussion of the *Readers' Guide* is drawn from Esther J. Bone, *"The Readers' Guide to Periodical Literature:* A Study" (MLS thesis, Kent State University, 1965); Frances W. Cheney, *Fundamental Reference Sources* (Chicago: American Library Association, 1971); and Paul Vesenyi, *An Introduction to Periodical Bibliography* (Ann Arbor, Mich.: Pierean Press, 1974).

2. The 106 articles in the sample are listed in the bibliography with an RG after the entry.

3. "If Pot Were Legal," *Time,* 20 July 1970, p. 41; "Pot and Sexuality," *Newsweek,* 29 April 1974, p. 57.

4. Richard J. Bonnie and Charles Whitebread II, *The Marihuana Conviction* (Charlottesville: University of Virginia Press, 1974); David F. Musto, *The American Disease* (New Haven: Yale University Press, 1973); Rufus King, *The Drug Hangup* (Springfield, Ill.: Charles Thomas, 1974); Erich Goode, ed., *Marihuana* (New York: Atherton Press, 1970); Stanley E. Grupp, ed., *Marihuana* (Columbus, Ohio: Charles E. Merrill, 1971); and K. Austin Kerr, *The Politics of Moral Behavior* (Reading, Mass.: Addison-Wesley, 1973). A full list of the hearings and reports studied is included in the bibliography.

5. King, *Drug Hang-up.*

BIBLIOGRAPHY

Articles from the *Readers' Guide* content study are included in this bibliography and followed by the initials RG. Government documents are listed under "U.S."

Adams, Roger. "Marihuana." *Science,* 9 August 1940, pp. 115-119. RG
"Aggressiveness and Pot." *Science Digest,* January 1976, p. 19. RG
Alexander, Shana. "The Case of the Pot-Smoking School Principal." *Life,* 17 November 1967, p. 25. RG
Allentuck, Samuel, and Bowman, Karl. "The Psychiatric Aspects of Marihuana Intoxication." *American Journal of Psychiatry* 99 (1942): 248-250.
Anslinger, Harry J., and Cooper, Courtney R. "Marihuana: Assassin of Youth." *American Magazine,* July 1937, pp. 18-19, 150-153. RG
Armagnac, Alden P. "Plant Wizards Fight Wartime Drug Peril." *Popular Science,* September 1943, pp. 62-63. RG
"Army Study of Marihuana Smokers Points to Better Ways of Treatment." *Newsweek,* 15 January 1945, pp. 72-74. RG
"As Common as Chewing Gum." *Time,* 1 March 1971, pp. 14-15. RG
Beck, Clarence W. "Marijuana Menace." *Literary Digest,* 1 January 1938, p. 26. RG
Beckelhymer, Hunter. "Grams and Damns." *Christian Century,* 4 March 1970, pp. 267-268. RG
Becker, Howard S. *Outsiders: Studies in the Sociology of Deviance.* New York: Free Press, 1963.

"Being Unbusted." *Time,* 17 July 1972, p. 50. RG

Berg, Roland H. "Warning: Steer Clear of THC." *Look,* 15 April 1969, p. 46. RG

Blum, Richard H., and Associates. *Utopiates.* New York: Atherton Press, 1964.

————. *Society and Drugs.* San Francisco: Jossey-Bass, 1969.

Bonnie, Richard J., and Whitebread, Charles II. "History of Marihuana Legislation." In *Marihuana: A Signal of Misunderstanding,* edited by the National Commission on Marihuana and Drug Abuse. Washington, D.C.: U.S. Government Printing Office, 1972. Appendix I, pp. 491-498.

————. *The Marihuana Conviction: A History of Marihuana Prohibition in the United States.* Charlottesville: University of Virginia, 1974.

"Boston Tea Party." *The New Republic,* 21 December 1968, p. 8. RG

Bourjaily, Vance. "Marijuana Politics: Iowa, 1973." *Harpers,* August 1973, pp. 12-14. RG

Brecher, Edward M., and the editors of *Consumer Reports. Licit and Illicit Drugs.* Boston: Little, Brown, 1972.

————. "Marijuana: The Health Questions." *Consumer Reports,* March 1975, pp. 143-149. RG

Brill, Henry. "Recurrent Patterns in the History of Drug Dependence and Some Interpretations." In *Drugs and Youth: Proceedings of the Rutgers Symposium on Drug Abuse,* edited by John Richard Wittenborn, pp. 8-25. Springfield, Illinois: Charles Thomas, 1969.

Bromberg, Walter. "Marihuana Intoxication." *American Journal of Psychiatry* 91 (1934):303-330.

Brotman, Richard, et al. "Drug Use Among Affluent High School Youth." In *Marijuana,* edited by Erich Goode, pp. 128-135. New York: Atherton, 1970.

Brotman, Richard, and Suffet, Frederic. "Marijuana Use: Values, Behavioral Definitions and Social Control." In *Drug Use in America,* edited by the National Commission on Marihuana and Drug Abuse. Washington, D.C.: U.S. Government Printing Office, 1973. Appendix I, pp. 1078-1110.

Brown, Clair A. "Marihuana." *Nature,* May 1938, pp. 271-272. RG

Buckley, William F., Jr. "Private Enterprise and Dope." *National Review,* 8 September 1970, p. 964. RG

————. "End the Pot Penalties." *Washington Star-News,* 10 November 1974.

Burke, Kenneth. *The Philosophy of Literary Form.* New York: Vintage, 1957.

California Division of Narcotics Enforcement. *Marihuana—Our Newest*

Narcotic Menace. Sacramento: California State Printing Office, 1939.

Cook, Shirley J. *Variations in Response to Illegal Drug Use.* Toronto: Alcoholism and Drug Addiction Research Foundation, 1970.

Cowan, Richard. "American Conservatives Should Revise Their Position on Marihuana." *National Review,* 8 December 1972, pp. 1344-1346.

Crancer, Alfred, et al. "Comparison of the Effects of Marihuana and Alcohol on Simulated Driving Performance." *Science,* 16 May 1969, pp. 851-854. RG

Crawford, Kenneth. "Vogues in Vice." *Newsweek,* 10 November 1969, p. 45. RG

"Crime of Marihuana." *The New Republic,* 7 October 1967, pp. 9-10. RG

"Danger." *Survey Graphic,* April 1938, p. 221. RG

Dickson, Donald T. "Bureaucracy and Morality." *Social Problems* 16 (1968):143-156.

Duster, Troy. *The Legislation of Morality.* New York: Free Press, 1970.

Einstein, Stanley, ed. *Proceedings of the First International Conference on Student Drug Surveys.* Farmingdale, N.Y.: Baywood, 1972.

Emboden, William A., Jr. "Ritual Use of Cannabis Sativa: A Historical Ethnographic Survey." In *The Flesh of the Gods,* edited by Peter Furst, pp. 214-236. New York: Praeger, 1972.

"Facts and Fancies About Marihuana." *Literary Digest,* 24 October 1936, pp. 7-8. RG

Fort, Joel. "Giver of Delight or Liberator of Sin: Drug Use and 'Addiction' in Asia." *Bulletin on Narcotics* 17, no. 3 (1965): 1-11 and 17; no. 4 (1965):13-19.

————. *The Pleasure Seekers.* New York: Grove Press, 1969.

————. "Drug Use and the Law: A Case for Legalizing Marijuana." *Current,* December 1969, pp. 4-13. RG

Fossier, A. E. "The Marihuana Menace." *New Orleans Medical and Surgical Journal* 84 (1931):247-252. Reprinted in U.S., Senate, Committee on the Judiciary, *Marihuana Decriminalization,* 94th Cong., 1st sess., 1975, pp. 675-676.

Frank, Arthur, and Frank, Stuart. "Marijuana." *Mademoiselle,* May 1975, pp. 22, 74. RG

"Fresh Disclosures on Drugs and GIs." *U.S. News & World Report,* 6 April 1970, pp. 32-33. RG

Galliher, John F.; McCartney, James L.; and Baum, Barbara. "Nebraska's Marihuana Law: A Case of Unexpected Legislative Innovation." *Law and Society Review* 8 (1974):441-456.

Galliher, John F., and Walker, Allyn. "The Puzzle of the Social Origins of the Marihuana Tax Act of 1937." *Social Problems* 24 (1977): 367-376.

Galliher, John F., and Basilick, Linda. "Utah's Liberal Drug Laws: Structural Foundations and Triggering Events." *Social Problems* 26 (1979):284-297.

Gard, Wayne. "Youth Gone Loco." *The Christian Century,* 29 June 1938, pp. 812-813. RG

Geertz, Clifford. "Ideology as a Cultural System." In *The Interpretation of Cultures,* pp. 193-233. New York: Basic Books, 1973.

Geis, Gilbert. "Social and Epidemiological Aspects of Marijuana Use." In *The New Social Drug,* edited by David Smith, pp. 78-90. Englewood Cliffs, New Jersey: Prentice-Hall, 1970.

"Getting Tough with Pot." *Time,* 8 December 1967, p. 110. RG

Ginsberg, Allen. "The Great Marihuana Hoax." *The Atlantic Monthly,* November 1966, pp. 104, 107-112. RG

Goffman, Erving. *Asylums.* Garden City, New York: Doubleday, 1961.

Goldberg, Melvin J. "A Father's Frank Talk About Marijuana." *Good Housekeeping,* February 1968, pp. 80-81. RG

Gollan, Antoni. "The Great Marihuana Problem." *National Review,* 30 January 1968, pp. 74-80. RG

Gomila, Frank, and Lambou, Madeline. "Present Status of the Marihuana Vice in the United States." In *Marihuana,* edited by Robert P. Walton, pp. 27-39. Philadelphia: J. B. Lippincott, 1938.

Goode, Erich. "Marijuana and the Politics of Reality." In *The New Social Drug,* edited by David Smith, pp. 168-186. Englewood Cliffs, New Jersey: Prentice-Hall, 1970.

_____.*Drugs in American Society.* New York: Knopf, 1972.

_____, ed. *Marijuana.* New York: Atherton Press, 1970.

Grinspoon, Lester. "Marihuana." *Scientific American,* December 1969, pp. 17-25. RG

_____.*Marihuana Reconsidered.* New York: Bantam, 1971.

Grupp, Stanley E., ed. *Marihuana.* Columbus, Ohio: Charles E. Merrill, 1971.

Gusfield, Joseph R. *Symbolic Crusade.* Urbana: University of Illinois Press, 1963.

_____. "Moral Passages: The Symbolic Process in Public Designations of Deviance." In *Law and the Behavioral Sciences,* edited by Lawrence M. Friedman and Stewart Macaulay, pp. 308-326. Indianapolis: Bobbs-Merrill, 1969.

Hart, Jeffrey. "Marihuana and the Counter Culture." *National Review,* 8 December 1972, p. 1348.

Helmer, John. *Drugs and Minority Oppression.* New York: Seabury Press, 1975.

Helmer, John, and Vietorisz, Thomas. *Drug Use, the Labor Market, and Class Conflict.* Washington, D.C.: Drug Abuse Council, 1974.

"Hemp Menace." *Business Week,* 12 January 1946, pp. 48-50. RG

Hering, Millicent B. "The Law and Maryjane." *American Libraries,* October 1970, pp. 896-899. RG

Himmelstein, Jerome L. "Drug Politics Theory: Analysis and Critique." *Journal of Drug Issues* 8 (1978):37-52.

"How Dangerous Is Marihuana? A Top Official Sparks New Debate." *U.S. News & World Report,* 30 October 1967, p. 20. RG

"If Pot Were Legal." *Time,* 20 July 1970, p. 41. RG

Jaeger, Gertrude, and Selznick, Philip. "A Normative Theory of Culture." *American Sociological Review* 29 (1964):653-669.

Jarvis, Scudamore, "Hashish Smugglers of Egypt." *Asia,* June 1930, pp. 440-444. RG

_____. "Hashish Smuggling in Egypt." *The Living Age,* January 1938, pp. 442-447. RG

Kaplan, John. *Marijuana—The New Prohibition.* New York: World Publishing, 1970.

"Keep off the Grass, HEW Warns." *Senior Scholastic,* 16 January 1975, p. 16. RG

Kerr, K. Austin. *The Politics of Moral Behavior: Prohibition and Drug Abuse.* Reading, Massachusetts: Addison-Wesley, 1973.

Kilpatrick, James J. "Thoughts on Marihuana." *Washington Star-News,* 4 December 1974.

King, Maxwell. "The Wild Hemp of Indiana." *The Nation,* 26 October 1970, pp. 402-403. RG

King, Rufus. *The Drug Hang-up.* Springfield, Illinois: Charles Thomas, 1974.

"Last week was a bad week for the narcs." *Science News,* 19 February 1972, pp. 117-118. RG

Leach, Henry G. "One More Peril for Youth." *Forum and Century,* January 1939, pp. 1-2. RG

Levine, Harry G. "Demon of the Middle Class: Self-control, Liquor, and the Ideology of Temperance in 19th-century America." Ph.D. diss., University of California, Berkeley, 1978.

Levine, Harvey R. *Legal Dimensions of Drug Abuse in the United States.* Springfield, Illinois: Charles Thomas, 1974.

Lewin, Louis. *Phantastica.* 1924; reprint ed., translated by P.H.A. Worth. New York: E. P. Dutton, 1964.

Lewis, Alfred H. "Marihuana." *Cosmopolitan,* October 1913, pp. 645-655. RG

Lindesmith, Alfred. *The Addict and the Law.* New York: Random House, 1965.

Livingston, Robert, ed. *History of Narcotic Drug Addiction Problems.* Washington, D.C.: Public Health Service, 1958.

McBroom, Patricia. " 'Pot' Penalties Too Severe." *Science,* 8 October 1966, p. 270. RG

McCormack, George R. "Marihuana." *Hygeia,* October 1937, pp. 898-899. RG

McCracken, Samuel. "The Drugs of Habit and the Drugs of Belief." *Commentary,* June 1971, pp. 43-52. RG

Mandel, Jerry. "Hashish, Assassins, and the Love of God." *Issues in Criminology* 2 (1966):149-156.

Margetts, Susan. "The Pot-Smoking Young Executives." *Dun's,* February 1970, pp. 42-43. RG

"Marihuana." *Journal of Home Economics,* September 1938, pp. 477-479. RG

"Marihuana and Memory." *Science,* 7 April 1972, p. 8. RG

"Marihuana Found Useful in Certain Ills." *Science News Letter,* 30 May 1942, p. 341. RG

"Marihuana Gives Some a Jag." *Science News Letter,* 14 January 1939, p. 30. RG

"Marihuana may lurk in window boxes." *Science News Letter,* 28 July 1951, p. 60. RG

"Marihuana Menaces Youth." *Scientific American,* March 1936, pp. 150-151. RG

"Marihuana: Millions of Turned-on Users." *Life,* 7 July 1967, pp. 16-23. RG

"Marihuana More Dangerous Than Heroin or Cocaine." *Scientific American,* May 1938, p. 293. RG

"Marihuana Smoking Seen as Epidemic Among the Idle." *Science News Letter,* 26 November 1938, p. 340. RG

"Marihuana Weed Grows Where Rope Factory Failed." *Science News Letter,* 15 January 1938, pp. 38-39. RG

"Marijuana and Mentality." *Newsweek,* 18 November 1946, pp. 70-72. RG

"Marijuana Commission finds usage high." *Science News,* 29 January 1972, p. 72. RG

"Marijuana: Cultural and Clinical Studies." *Science News,* 13 December 1975, p. 374. RG

"Marijuana Is Still Illegal." *Time,* 29 December 1967, p. 38. RG

"Marines and Marihuana." *Newsweek,* 31 December 1951, p. 17. RG

Marshall, Maud A. "Marihuana." *American Scholar,* January 1939, pp. 95-101. RG

Maurer, David W. "Marijuana Addicts and Their Lingo." *American Mercury,* November 1946, pp. 571-575. RG

Mawer, E. B. "Hachisch Eating." *Cornhill Magazine,* May 1894, pp. 500-505. RG

Mechoulam, Raphael. "Marihuana Chemistry." *Science,* 5 June 1970, pp. 1159-1166. RG

"Menace of Marihuana." *Science Digest,* July 1945, pp. 49-50. RG

"Mild Intoxicant." *Scientific American,* February 1969, pp. 42-43. RG

"Morality of Marijuana." *Time,* 16 August 1968, p. 58. RG

"More Controversy About Pot." *Time,* 31 May 1971, p. 65. RG

Morgan, Patricia A. "The Legislation of Drug Laws: Economic Crisis and Social Control." *Journal of Drug Issues* 8 (1978):53-62.

————. "The Political Uses of Moral Reform: California and Federal Drug Policy, 1910-1960." Ph.D. diss., University of California, Santa Barbara, 1978.

Musto, David F. "The Marihuana Tax Act of 1937." *Archives of General Psychiatry* 26 (1972):101-108.

————. *The American Disease: Origins of Narcotics Control.* New Haven: Yale University Press, 1973.

"Narcotics and the Law." *Commonweal,* August 1961, pp. 467-469. RG

National Organization for the Reform of Marihuana Laws. "The Marihuana Issue." 1977, p. 12.

"New Federal Tax Hits Dealings in Potent Weed." *Newsweek,* 14 August 1937, pp. 22-23. RG

New York City Mayor's Committee on Marihuana. "The Marihuana Problem in the City of New York." In *The Marihuana Papers,* edited by David Solomon, pp. 277-410. New York: New American Library, 1966.

Oberdeck, S. K. "Problems of Pot." *National Review,* 1 June 1971, p. 597. RG

Odegard, Peter. *Pressure Politics.* New York: Columbia University Press, 1928.

"Of Pot and Rats." *Time,* 27 September 1971, p. 71. RG

Oteri, Joseph S., and Silvergate, Harvey A. "In the Marketplace of Free Ideas: A Look at the Passage of the Marihuana Tax Act." In *Marihuana: Myths and Realities,* edited by J. L. Simmons, pp. 136-162. North Hollywood: Brandon House, 1967.

"Our Home Hasheesh Crop." *Literary Digest,* 3 April 1926, pp. 64-65. RG

Pan, Lynn. *Alcohol in Colonial Africa.* Helsinki: Finnish Foundation for Alcohol Studies, 1975.

Parry, Albert. "The Menace of Marihuana." *The American Mercury,* December 1935, pp. 487-490. RG

"Picking off Pot Stickers." *Newsweek,* 18 October 1976, p. 13. RG

"Pinning Down the Weed." *Science News,* 27 September 1969, pp. 263-264. RG

Polsky, Ned. "The Village Beat Scene: Summer, 1960." In *Hustlers, Beats, and Others,* pp. 144-182. Garden City, New York: Doubleday, 1969.

Price, Thomas, and Hargraves, Ruth. "Decriminalization of Marijuana: Dealing with the Reality, not the Symbol." *Christian Century,* 4 September 1974, pp. 822-823. RG

"Pot and Sex." *Time,* 29 September 1975, p. 54. RG

"Pot and Sexuality." *Newsweek,* 29 April 1974, p. 57. RG

"Pot-Picking Time." *Newsweek,* 17 May 1965, p. 42. RG

"Pot Pourri." *Family Health,* July 1976, p. 22. RG

"Pot Problem." *Time,* 12 March 1965, p. 49. RG

Powelson, Harvey. "Marijuana: More Dangerous Than You Think." *Reader's Digest,* December 1974, pp. 95-99. RG

"Questioning the Legal Status." *Science News,* 22 May 1971, p. 349. RG

Rafaelson, Ole J. "Cannabis and Alcohol: Effects on Simulated Car Driving." *Science,* 2 March 1973, pp. 920-923. RG

"Reefers on KPFA." *Newsweek,* 10 May 1954, p. 92. RG

"Reports on Opium and Hemp." *Spectator,* 27 April 1895, pp. 570-571. RG

Robinson, Edward Forbes. *The Early History of Coffee Houses in England.* London: Kegan Paul, 1893.

Rosenthal, Franz. *The Herb: Hashish Versus Medieval Muslim Society.* Leiden: E. J. Brill, 1977.

Rosenthal, Michael P. "The Legislative Response to Marihuana: When the Shoe Pinches Enough." *Journal of Drug Issues* 7 (1977):61-77.

Rowell, Earl A., and Rowell, Robert. *On the Trail of Marihuana: The Weed of Madness.* Mountain View, Calif.: Pacific Press, 1939.

"Saw-toothed." *New Yorker,* 11 August 1951, pp. 18-19. RG

Schroeder, Richard C. *The Politics of Drugs.* 2d rev. ed. Washington, D.C.: Congressional Quarterly, 1980.

Schultes, Richard E. "Man and Marihuana." *Natural History* 82 (1973): 58-63.

Scripture, Edward W. "Consciousness Under the Influence of Cannabis." *Science,* 27 October 1893, pp. 233-234. RG

Simon, Carlton. "From Opium to Hash Eesh: Startling Facts Regarding the Narcotics Evil and Its Many Ramifications Throughout the World." *Scientific American,* November 1921, pp. 14-15. RG

Skolnick, Jerome H. "Coercion to Virtue: The Enforcement of Morals." *Southern California Law Review* 41 (1968):588-641.

Smith, David, ed. *The New Social Drug.* Englewood Cliffs, New Jersey: Prentice-Hall, 1970.

Smith, Roger. "U.S. Marihuana Legislation and the Creation of a Social

Powelson Harvey

Reader's Digest 1974

erso

ith

io en la lengua española

estrella a la vida

molécula al hombre

rera

Problem." In *The New Social Drug,* edited by David Smith, pp. 105-117. Englewood Cliffs, New Jersey: Prentice-Hall, 1970.

Snider, Arthur J. "Drug Dangers: The Case Gets Stronger." *Science Digest,* July 1968, pp. 62-63. RG

Snyder, Solomon H. "What We Have Forgotten About Pot—A Pharmacologist's History." *New York Times Magazine,* 13 December 1970, pp. 26-27. RG

Solomon, David, ed. *The Marihuana Papers.* New York: New American Library, 1966.

Spock, Benjamin. "Preventing Drug Abuse in Children." *Redbook,* May 1971, p. 36. RG

Stanley, Eugene. "Marihuana as a Developer of Criminals." *Journal of Police Science* 2 (1931):256. Reprinted in U.S., Senate, Committee on the Judiciary, 94th Cong., 1st sess., *Marijuana Decriminalization,* 1975, pp. 624-633.

Taylor, Norman. *Flight From Reality.* New York: Duell, Sloan, and Pearce, 1949.

Terry, Charles E., et al. "Report of the Committee on Habit-forming Drugs." *American Journal of Public Health* 13 (1923):39-41.

Terry, Charles E., and Pellens, Mildred. *The Opium Problem.* 1928; reprint ed., Montclair, New Jersey: Patterson Smith, 1970.

"Tests Show Marihuana Does Not Help." *Science News Letter,* 29 April 1944, pp. 278-279. RG

"The History of Marihuana." *Newsweek,* 28 November 1938, p. 29. RG

"The Latest Medical Facts About Marihuana." *Good Housekeeping,* May 1971, pp. 185-186. RG

"The Weed." *Time,* 19 July 1943, pp. 54-56. RG

"To Parents: Plain Talk on Marijuana." *Business Week,* 21 March 1970, p. 121. RG

U.S. Canal Zone Governor. *Annual Report of the Governor of the Panama Canal Zone.* Washington, D.C.: U.S. Government Printing Office, 1923-1930.

U.S. Federal Bureau of Narcotics. *Traffic in Opium and Other Dangerous Drugs.* Washington, D.C.: U.S. Government Printing Office, 1926-1962.

U.S. House of Representatives, Committee on Interstate and Foreign Commerce, Subcommittee on Public Health and Welfare. *Increased Control Over Hallucinogens and Other Dangerous Drugs.* 90th Cong., 2d sess., 1968.

U.S. House of Representatives, Committee on Interstate and Foreign Commerce, Subcommittee on Public Health and Welfare. *Drug Abuse Control Amendments—1970.* 91st Cong., 2d sess., 1970.

U.S. House of Representatives, Committee on Ways and Means. *Taxation of Marihuana.* 75th Cong., 1st sess., 1937.

U.S. House of Representatives, Committee on Ways and Means. *Control of Narcotics, Marijuana, and Barbiturates.* 82d Cong., 1st sess., 1951.

U.S. House of Representatives, Committee on Ways and Means. *Traffic in, and Control of, Narcotics, Barbiturates, and Amphetamines.* 84th Cong., 1956.

U.S. House of Representatives, Committee on Ways and Means. *Controlled Dangerous Substances, Narcotics, and Drug Control Laws.* 91st Cong., 2d sess., 1970.

U.S. House of Representatives, Select Committee on Crime. *Crime in America—Drug Abuse and Criminal Justice.* 91st Cong., 1st sess., 1969.

U.S. House of Representatives, Select Committee on Crime. *Crime in America—Views on Marihuana.* 91st Cong., 1st sess., 1969.

U.S. National Commission on Law Observance and Enforcement. *Report on Crime and the Foreign Born.* Washington, D.C.: U.S. Government Printing Office, 1931.

U.S. National Commission on Marihuana and Drug Abuse. *Marihuana: A Signal of Misunderstanding.* Washington, D.C.: U.S. Government Printing Office, 1972.

U.S. National Commission on Marihuana and Drug Abuse. *Drug Use in America: Problem in Perspective.* Washington, D.C.: U.S. Government Printing Office, 1973.

U.S. National Institute on Drug Abuse. *Marihuana and Health.* Washington, D.C.: U.S. Government Printing Office, 1971-1976.

U.S. President's Ad Hoc Panel on Drug Abuse. *Progress Report.* Washington, D.C.: U.S. Government Printing Office, 1962.

U.S. President's Advisory Commission on Narcotic and Drug Abuse. *Final Report.* Washington, D.C.: U.S. Government Printing Office, 1963.

U.S. President's Commission on Law Enforcement and Administration of Justice. *Task Force: Narcotics and Drug Abuse.* Washington, D.C.: U.S. Government Printing Office, 1967.

U.S. Senate, Committee on Finance. *Taxation of Marihuana.* 75th Cong., 1st sess., 1937.

U.S. Senate, Committee on Government Operations. *Organized Crime and Illicit Traffic in Narcotics.* 88th Cong., 1963-1964.

U.S. Senate, Committee on the Judiciary. *Narcotics Control Act of 1956.* 84th Cong., 2d sess., 1956.

U.S. Senate, Committee on the Judiciary. *Narcotic Rehabilitation Act of 1966.* 89th Cong., 2d sess., 1966.

U.S. Senate, Committee on the Judiciary. *Marijuana Decriminalization.* 94th Cong., 1st sess., 1975.

U.S. Senate, Committee on the Judiciary, Subcommittee on Improvements in the Federal Criminal Code. *Illicit Narcotics Traffic.* 84th Cong., 1955-1956.

U.S. Senate, Committee on the Judiciary, Subcommittee to Investigate the Administration of the Internal Security Act and Other Internal Security Laws. *Marihuana-Hashish Epidemic and Its Impact on United States Security.* 94th Cong., 1st sess., 1975.

U.S. Senate, Committee on the Judiciary, Subcommittee to Investigate Juvenile Delinquency. *Juvenile Delinquency.* 86th Cong., 2d sess., 1960; 87th Cong., 2d sess., 1962; 90th Cong., 2d sess., 1968.

U.S. Senate, Committee on the Judiciary, Subcommittee to Investigate Juvenile Delinquency. *Narcotic Legislation.* 91st Cong., 1st sess., 1969.

U.S. Senate, Committee on Labor and Public Welfare, Subcommittee on Alcoholism and Narcotics. *Narcotics Addiction and Drug Abuse.* 91st Cong., 1st sess., 1969.

U.S. Senate, Committee on Labor and Public Welfare, Special Subcommittee on Alcoholism and Narcotics. *Federal Drug Abuse and Drug Dependence Prevention, Treatment, and Rehabilitation Act of 1970.* 91st Cong., 2d sess., 1970.

U.S. Senate, Special Committee to Investigate Organized Crime in Interstate Commerce. *Organized Crime in Interstate Commerce.* 81st Cong., 2d sess., 1950.

Walton, Robert P. *Marihuana: America's New Drug Problem.* Philadelphia: J. B. Lippincott, 1938.

————. "The Marihuana Problem." *Science,* 25 May 1945, pp. 538-539. RG

Weil, Andrew T.; Zinberg, Norman E.; and Nelson, Judith M. "Clinical and Psychological Effects of Marijuana in Man." *Science,* 13 December 1968, pp. 1234-1242. RG

"What Happens to Marihuana Smokers." *Science Digest,* May 1945, pp. 35-40. RG

"What? Pot? Not Laredo." *Forbes,* 1 November 1970, p. 48. RG

White House Conference on Narcotic and Drug Abuse. *Proceedings.* Washington, D.C.: U.S. Government Printing Office, 1962.

"Wicked Weed." *Science Digest,* April 1952, p. 48. RG

Wilson, Earl. "Crazy Dreamers." *Collier's,* 4 June 1949, p. 27. RG

Winters, S. R. "Marihuana." *Hygeia,* October 1940, pp. 885-887. RG

Wolf, William. "Uncle Sam Fights a New Drug Menace. . . Marijuana." *Popular Science Monthly,* May 1936, pp. 14-15. RG

INDEX

About the Author

JEROME L. HIMMELSTEIN is currently Assistant Professor of Sociology at Amherst College. He received his Ph.D. in Sociology from the University of California, Berkeley, and was a postdoctoral fellow at the Center for Research on Social Organization at the University of Michigan, Ann Arbor. His writings have appeared in *Society*, the *American Journal of Sociology*, *The Psychoanalytic Review*, the *International Journal of Addictions*, the *Journal of Drug Issues*, and *Contemporary Crises*.